SOMETHING OF GREAT CONSTANCY

A reading of Shakespeare's
A Midsummer Night's Dream

Matt Simpson

For Peter —

Thanks for the good conversation —

Matt

24·04·07

GE

GREENWICH EXCHANGE
LONDON

Greenwich Exchange, London

First published in Great Britain in 2006
All rights reserved

Something of Great Constancy
A Reading of Shakespeare's *A Midsummer Night's Dream*
© Matt Simpson 2006

Printed and bound by Q3 Digital/Litho, Loughborough
Tel: 01509 213456
Typesetting and layout by Albion Associates, London
Tel: 020 8852 4646
Cover design by December Publications, Belfast
Tel: 028 90286559

Cover picture: © ArenaPAL

Greenwich Exchange Website: www.greenex.co.uk

ISBN-13: 978-1-871551-90-7
ISBN-10: 1-871551-90-0

for Angela Topping

I would like to express my gratitude to John Farrell who listened to some of my ideas, to the dedicatee of this study, Angela Topping, who helped sharpen them, and, as ever, to Professor John Lucas for reading the typescript and invaluable suggestions.

Already with thee! tender is the night,
And haply the Queen-Moon is on her throne,
Clustered around by all her starry fays.
John Keats

Queen and huntress, chaste and fair,
* Now the sun is laid to sleep,*
Seated in thy silver chair,
* State in wonted manner keep;*
*   Hesperus entreats thy light,*
*   Goddess excellently bright.*

Earth, let not thy envious shade
* Dare itself to interpose;*
Cynthia's shining orb was made
* Heaven to clear the day did close;*
*   Bless us then with wishèd sight,*
*   Goddess excellently bright.*

Lay thy bow of pearl apart,
* And thy crystal-shing quiver;*
Give unto the flying hart
* Space to breathe, how short soever;*
*   Thou that mak'st day of night –*
*   Goddess excellently bright.*
Ben Jonson

* Tell me where is fancy bred,*
Or in the heart, or in the head?
How begot, how nourishèd?
*   Reply, reply.*
It is engend'red in the eyes,
With gazing fed ...
The Merchant of Venice

*   Earth's the right place for love;*
I don't know where it's likely to go better.
Robert Frost

Contents

Prologue – A Play Toward

Shakespeare, more than any other writer, comes loaded with history. By this I mean he brings a four-hundred-year-large crowd with him – stage directors, critics, teachers, students – all jostling to make known their views about his work. And sometimes Shakespeare gets lost in the babble of competing voices. In a sense, and because of this, we can end up knowing the plays, to use words of Othello, not wisely but too well. Put at its simplest, we often know what is going to happen. A consequence being, for instance, that in *Hamlet* audiences sit in anticipation of how the hero is going to deliver the line "To be, or not to be, that is the question". Or, again, in *The Winter's Tale*, we know the statue *is* Hermione and therefore, unless we are in a willing suspension of disbelief, miss out on an intense moment of theatrical astonishment. There is no way out of this. The process of recovery, re-interpretation, has to and will go on, and will always, inevitably, be subject to fashion and prevailing tastes. As a result, however, we of necessity forfeit what music presenters call the innocent ear, the experience of hearing or seeing something for the first time. We may also encounter distortion or be drawn in to excessively admiring the virtuosity of performers over the art they are there to mediate to us. We live in what D.H. Lawrence once excoriated as "these personal times", what that fine poet W.D. Jackson recently characterised as "the ruthless and materialistic individualism" of our age.

It is a truism that every generation has its *Hamlet*: people talk of Olivier's *Hamlet*, the 'Russian' *Hamlet*, Peter Brook's, Mel Gibson's, Ethan Hawk's and so on – much in the same way they talk of Rattle's or Harnoncourt's Beethoven. An interesting game I find is to ask what book Hamlet enters reading in Act II. In the play's first production it seems fairly obvious he is reading Montaigne's *Essays.*

When I was a student, it would have been something by Sartre or Camus, his stage director would have been Jan Kott (or influenced by him), he would have worn a black leather jacket and been politically motivated. Hard to say what he would be reading today: Stephen Hawking … or maybe Stephen King? Would he be politically cynical, euphorically alcoholic, atheistic, wear a baseball cap, be electronically educated?

We talk variously of psychological, political, religious, feminist interpretations of the plays, depending on particular theoretical stances we take or are taken by a director or critic. Critics argue with one another and directors tend to foreground particular aspects (Olivier's *Hamlet* was for instance Freudian): sometimes this shines a light on the play, sometimes it can seem wilful distortion. One of the purposes of criticism is to make us aware and so be chary of partial interpretations and to go some way towards getting nearer to the heart of a play. Of course this is idealistic. It implies something of Miranda's vision in *The Tempest* of the brave new world represented to her sight by the appearance for the first time of human creatures other than her father and the debased Caliban. John Middleton Murry, pondering possible connections between *A Midsummer Night's Dream* and the English Court, has remarked:

> We incline to say to ourselves that the dewy beauty which pearls *A Midsummer Night's Dream* can never have been intended for a popular audience. That is, I believe, because we have no experience of what a truly naïve performance of the *Dream* might be.

Murry isn't, I'm sure, using the word "naïve" in a negative sense but simply reminding us of imagining – or trying to – as far as humanly possible, something of what the play's first audiences may have experienced. Naturally many things get in the way of this but the job is to make some kind of approximation. Few would argue now that the Authentic Performance movement in music hasn't – to mix metaphors – stripped away layers of dust and varnish. What we are attempting to do then is to make an effort in the direction of what Eliot called the historical imagination and see something of what may actually be there in the play.

Part of the baggage *A Midsummer Night's Dream* carries is its associations with Victorian and Edwardian depictions of fairy by painters and illustrators of children's books. (Many Edwardians were duped by cod photographs of fairies taken by the two young girls, Frances Griffiths and Elsie Wright, of Cotingley in Yorkshire). What we tend to get, then, is a mix of the sentimental, the twee, the grotesque, along with a kind of disguised or submerged eroticism. Mendelssohn's incidental music, brilliant though it is, has not always helped in the ways in which we perceive the play and how it works. Productions as a result can even now be overloaded with gauzy wings, pretty flowers, trees, over-elaborate scenery – what Stanley Wells in his Introduction to the *Penguin Shakespeare* calls the "pictorial, quasi-operatic style of production". Inevitable reaction to this airy-fairyness (the presentation of fairies on stage remains problematic) began in this country in the early years of the 20th century with directors like Harley Granville-Barker and has been salutary, but sometimes with the effect of throwing the baby out with the bath water.

For example, Jan Kott, in his influential *Shakespeare Our Contemporary* of 1964, sees the play as "most truthful, brutal, and violent ... the most erotic of Shakespeare's plays", its setting a drunken orgiastic party:

> It is late at night and the entertainment is over. All the toasts have been drunk, dancing has stopped. Servants are still holding lamps in the courtyard. But the adjoining garden is dark. Tightly embracing couples are slowly filtering through the gate. Spanish wine is heavy; the lovers have remained. Someone has passed by; the boy is waking up. He does not see the girl asleep by his side. He has forgotten everything, even that he left the dance with her. Another girl is near; to reach her it is enough for him to stretch his arm. He has stretched his arm, he runs after her. He hates now with an intensity equal to that with which an hour ago he desired.

I am not, of course, saying a production of this kind is invalid nor any of those mentioned in Jonathan Bate's *The Genius of Shakespeare*, like the Magdeburg staging in the 1970s, in which "the lovers' reintegration into society at the end of the play was viewed cynically", and the anti-Franco productions in Spain which "emphasized the power of youth to go against oppressive parental will and achieve freedom in the magical world of the forest". But what we need to ask is whether such interpretations illuminate or do damage – end up becoming something other than Shakespeare. It is all too easy to impose our modern cynicisms and risk vulgarising the plays. That said, Shakespeare's great strength lies in the fact his work is sufficiently multi-faceted to allow for and survive bad productions and bad performances. This is in no way to imply that *A Midsummer Night's Dream* is all innocent pantomime and doesn't, like the moon that dominates it, have a darker side. Lives are threatened with death and danger, friendship gets torn apart, Nature herself is shown as being in a state of catastrophic upheaval, and at the play's end midnight comes not only as a time for newly-weds to hurry off to their bride-beds but also as the witching hour when "the wolf behowls the moon" and

> the graves, all gaping wide,
> Every one lets forth his sprite
>
> (Act V, scene 1, 370-71)

That said, the play – described by Coleridge as "one continual specimen of dramatised lyrical" – seems to most people genial and comic and, in the scenes involving Bottom, unfailingly hilarious. Puck, for all his connections in folklore with the devil, is impish rather than malevolent, Jack gets his Jill, naught goes ill, and the moon and the fairies in the end fulfil their roles as protective spirits of both Nature and human endeavour. It strongly brings to mind the world of Blake's *Songs of Innocence and Experience*. Let me quote the one called *A Dream*:

> Once a dream did weave a shade
> O'er my Angel-guarded bed,
> That an emmet lost its way
> Where on grass methought I lay.
>
> Troubled, 'wilder'd, and forlorn,
> Dark, benighted, travel-worn,
> Over many a tangled spray,
> All heart-broke I heard her say:

"O, my children! Do they cry?
Do they hear their father sigh?
Now they look abroad to see:
Now return and weep for me."

Pitying, I drop'd a tear;
But I saw a glow-worm near,
Who replied: "What wailing wight
Calls the watchman of the night?

I am set to light the ground,
While the beetle goes his round:
Follow now the beetle's hum;
Little wanderer, hie thee home."

A Midsummer Night's Dream is in many ways a unique play. It is one of the few for which there is no immediate source. Ovid's presence is strongly felt in it and there are indications that Shakespeare has read his Plutarch and is perhaps faintly remembering his Chaucer (Theseus appears in *The Knight's Tale*), but the whole play, as far as we know, is of his own devising. The fairies conceived of as tiny creatures were his invention, even if bred out of his memories of the English countryside. He was experimenting confidently with making a beautifully symmetrical plot, putting contrasting groups together; in terms of poetry he was putting on a virtuoso performance. M.C. Bradbrook says:

> His first completely individual comedy was to remain, *sui generis*, a 'species' of which only one specimen was to be found in nature.

John Lucas, in his monograph on *The Winter's Tale* wisely recommends Samuel Johnson's writings on Shakespeare. The following extract indicates Johnson's general approach and represents something of what I am trying to live up to and recommend to students:

> The reader, I believe, is seldom pleased to find his opinion anticipated; it is natural to delight more in what we find or make, than in what we receive. Judgement, like other faculties,

is improved by practice, and its advancement is hindered by submission to dictatorial decisions, as is memory by the use of a table book. Some initiation is however necessary; of all skill, part is infused by precept, and part is obtained by habit; I have therefore shewn so much as may enable the candidate of criticism to discover the rest.

It would be gratifying to think this commentary might act as such an 'initiation' to the work of a great dramatist who, as Johnson observes, "approximates the remote, and familiarizes the wonderful".

1

The Silliest Stuff

In one of her comments on the Pyramus and Thisbe play, Hippolyta says "This is the silliest stuff that ever I heard". It is easy to misunderstand her words: "silly" carries a meaning lost to us. It does not necessarily mean childishly foolish or stupid but something more like unsophisticated, simple. In pastoral writing sheep are often referred to as "silly", which means no more than that they are innocent, simple, dumb animals. The phrase "in silly sooth" frequently used during the period had for its meaning: straightforward truth. Hippolyta is not being necessarily dismissive. In fact one could argue, if we allow the word to mean innocent, she is being complimentary. However, if we take her words as derogatory then they are only mildly so and earn a gentle rebuke: Theseus tells her "The best in this kind are but shadows; and the worst are no worse, if imagination amend them." His word "shadows" is a pun: actors were called shadows, and with it he draws attention to the fact that what the audience is witnessing is professional actors playing amateur actors playing parts. "It must be your imagination, then, and not theirs", is his wife's reply. He simply states, with princely munificence, "If we imagine no worse of them than they of themselves, they may pass for excellent men." There is a great deal of emphasis in *A Midsummer Night's Dream* on the transformative power of the imagination. It is one of the play's great preoccupations. Simplicity (the "naïve" quality Murry says we fail to experience) can, in a cynical age, be hard to handle: simplicity is a sophisticated thing, as, say, performers of Mozart will tell you, and which, as T.S. Eliot says, can cost "not less than everything". Shakespeare's purpose on the whole is benign: to provide audiences with pleasure, to make them laugh, dazzle them with poetry, with fast-moving action, interesting and amusing characters, and to make them feel, for at least the time the play takes, the world can be put right.

* * * * *

Dr Johnson tells us "Shakespeare with his excellencies has likewise faults" and for a moment I want to glance at some things in the play one may regard as anomalies.

At first sight *A Midsummer Night's Dream* is a hotchpotch of seemingly incongruous elements: classical mythology and native folklore, Athenian court and English wood, Athenian nobility with classical names and rude mechanicals with English names. To quote Johnson again, "He has no regard to distinction of time or place, but gives to one age or nation, without scruple, the customs, institutions, and opinions of another, at the expense not only of likelihood, but of possibility." The play also has a Christian underscoring which will become clear later.

None of this worries Shakespeare nor the audience he was writing for – though those purist critics who advocated adherence to classical rules or who, like Theseus, pride themselves on their rationality, inevitably level the charge of impurity at him or find excuses in terms of a rough-and-ready 'native genius'.

Let's point to these anomalies and then, perhaps, wisely shelve them.

First then, the play opens with the suggestion that the marriage between Theseus and Hippolyta will be solemnised in four days when in fact it takes place after two. Equally, in the first scene, Theseus says:

> Come, my Hippolyta. What cheer, my love?
> Demetrius and Egeus, go along;
> I must employ you in some business
> Against our nuptial, and confer with you
> Of something nearly that concerns yourselves.
>
> (Act I, scene 1, 122-6)

This conveniently and implausibly (though it might be argued he is taking Egeus and Demetrius aside to admonish them or get them to relent) leaves the two aberrant lovers, Lysander and Hermia, privately together to plan an elopement. It seems rash of Theseus and Egeus not to anticipate and guard against this happening. Then again, Shakespeare forgets he has Quince in Act I, scene 2, allot the parts of Thisbe's mother (Starveling), Pyramus' father (Snout), with himself to play the part of Thisbe's father ... that is unless we assume Philostrate, in his job as "manager of mirth", has vetted the play at rehearsal and actually reduced it to "some ten words long". The problematic business of the changeling boy will be tackled later. Oberon has Celtic origins (though Shakespeare may have known the name from other sources, such as Spenser's *The Fairie Queene*); Titania's origins are classical; Puck's English. Then there is the fact that in Act III, scene 2, Oberon tells Puck:

> I'll to my Queen and beg her Indian boy,
> And then I will her charmèd eye release
> From monster's view, and all things shall be peace.
> (Act III, scene 2, 375-7)

This presupposes that in her state of enchantment and infatuation with Bully Bottom she is either emotionally and/or rationally capable of entertaining a request which, so adamantly and with such disastrous natural consequences, she has up till now denied. But in Act IV, scene 1, we hear Oberon reporting:

> When I had at my pleasure taunted her,
> And she in mild terms begged my patience,
> I then did ask of her her changeling child,
> Which straight she gave me, and her fairy sent
> To bear him to my bower in Fairyland.
> And now I have the boy I will undo
> This hateful imperfection of her eyes.
> (Act IV, scene 1, 56-62)

What it is that makes her suddenly so compliant – especially while she is still in thrall to the love-juice – is not explained. There also remains the fact that, whilst the other lovers are released from enchantment, Demetrius is not – that is unless we accept Oberon's "When thou wakest, if she be by,/Beg of her for remedy" to signify that the power to release Demetrius from enchantment lies with

Helena. It, of course, makes the pairing-off of lovers neatly symmetrical and may be viewed as Shakespeare, as with previous instances, unashamedly working the plot. Maybe we are expected – and some people do – to think in terms of poetic justice: in other words Demetrius is *benevolently* given his deserts (or has been transformed into being his *real* self) and therefore no harm's done. There are no suggestions (unless we read one into Oberon's lines quoted above) that he will grow out of or eventually be released from this condition. He has, as it were, been genetically modified.

It is, of course, wrong to imagine existences outside the play. The play requires us to travel no further than the point of happily-ever-after and not for us to speculate on how successful the couplings celebrated in it may or may not turn out to be. We are simply to take on trust Oberon's:

> So shall all the couples three
> Ever true in loving be,
> And the blots of nature's hand
> Shall not in their issue stand.
>
> (Act V, scene 1, 397-400)

The purpose of the play's ending is to bless the couples and ensure their fertility so that:

> Jack shall have Jill;
> Naught shall go ill.
> The man shall have his mare again, and all shall be well.
>
> (Act III, scene 2, 461-3)

Another convenience to the plot is to have the 'mechanicals' rehearse in the wood. Quince asks them to:

> meet me in the palace wood a mile without the town
> by moonlight. There will we rehearse; for if we meet
> in the city we shall be dogged with company, and our
> devices known.
>
> (Act I, scene 2, 93-7)

Meeting in the evening (i.e. after work) makes sense but rehearsing in a wood in the dark stretches plausibility – whether the reasons for doing so are Quince's or Shakespeare's is another matter.

Yet again, Athens, looking forward to joyful wedding celebrations, is entirely unaware of the catastrophic condition of Nature revealed to us in Titania's long speech in Act II.

Then, in Act III, scene 2, Oberon instructs Puck to "overcast the night", a thing difficult if not impossible in a modern theatre (unless it's somehow managed in an outdoor production) or in the cinema or on a television screen where a degree of lighting is required if we are to make sense of what's happening. In the afternoon performances in Shakespeare's Globe the audience is obliged to let its imagination do the work.[1]

Finally we might just mention that, though Oberon and Titania are fully-grown beings, the smallness of Shakespeare's fairies also has to be imagined. (In some modern productions, they are played by children). In view of the preoccupation with the power of the imagination the play takes on board, this is no small point.

What I have termed anomalies normally become lost in the enchantment the play has us surrender to. It is not a realist drama. It is salutary to think Shakespeare may be offering a warning when he has Bottom say, "Man is but an ass if he go about to expound this dream".

Notes
[1]   See the Prologue to *Henry V*.

2

Love Can Transpose

… to dignity. It can also transpose to indignity, as we will discover. Love, in the courtly or Petrarchan mode (Shakespeare's young lovers tend to get their ideas from books)[1] is meant to ennoble (Pyramus kills himself for love) but more often than not performs quite the opposite function: it confuses the senses, maddens and makes sick, at worst reduces the lover to a bestial level. If the courtly mode of love is one of adoration and exaggerated compliment, we clearly see the opposite in the scenes where the lovers exchange insults and act decidedly ungallantly.

A Midsummer Night's Dream is a play of transformations – transposing, translating, transfiguring, transporting (these words are found in the play) – things changing from one condition to another and back again in altered form.

Transformation chimes with ways most people of the period seemed to have thought. It is useful to sketch something of this in here. According to the cosmology of the time, everything existing in the sublunary world (we will consider the vital importance of the moon in the next chapter) was subject to change and decay, as distinct from the celestial regions beyond, in which everything was eternal, change-less. Life for the Christian goes through a cycle of birth, growth, death, resurrection – from change to changelessness. It is important to view Shakespeare's plays as existing not just in the sublunary world but in the greater context of eternity – without which we miss a necessary dimension. The play brings immortals on to the stage and characters from the past to life. The multi-layered-ness of plot and meaning is also consonant with the analogical way of thinking of the time, the way all created things were linked in a matrix of correspondences.

A favourite book of Shakespeare's was the *Metamorphoses* of the Roman poet, Ovid, the impact of which, as well as Ovid's love poetry, not just on Shakespeare but on western European literature generally, cannot be overestimated. *Metamorphoses* was translated into English by Arthur Golding in 1565-7. Shakespeare knew his Ovid with enough intimacy to enable him, as we will see, to go as far as playfully drawing comic parallels.

There is a contemporary account of Shakespeare likening him to Ovid. We find it in *Palladis Tamia*, written in 1598 by Francis Meres, in which Meres declares:

> As the soul of Euphorbus was thought to live in Pythagoras: so the sweet witty soul of Ovid lives in mellifluous and honey-tongued Shakespeare.

In *A Midsummer Night's Dream* there are so many direct connections with Ovid's *Metamorphoses* (Maureen Duffy in her book *The Erotic World of Faery* has counted 26) it's usually assumed Shakespeare had Golding's translation on his desk at the time of writing. *Metamorphoses* is a long poem in 15 books, a collection of mythological stories, whose constant theme was the transformation of objects, animals, human beings into other forms – into trees, birds, rocks, etc. The gods in it are capricious and the collection is held together by the overarching theme of primal chaos being transformed to harmony. In other words, it represents, collectively, a creation myth.

A Midsummer Night's Dream is a play in which, to use words of Othello, chaos is come again – a play about the consequences of dissension (or, in Christian terms hinted at in the text, of original sin) and about trying to find "the concord of this discord".

The play is a pattern of transformations, movements from one state or condition to another and back again. The word "Midsummer" in the title indicates we are at a moment of crucial changes. The play takes us from day into night and back again into day and then to night again, from light to dark then back to light, from being awake to sleeping/dreaming then to re-awakening, from Athens to a wood and back to Athens, from civility to untamed nature and enchantment then again back to civility. Theseus and Hippolyta may be said to be transforming themselves by marriage; lovers' lives are altered by love and jealousy and undergo a whole variety of magical changes; they move from good sense through madness and/or being spellbound to re-emerge into the light of reason; ordinary folk turn themselves – albeit uncomfortably – into actors ("visions", "shadows"); Bottom is translated into an ass and then restored to his 'normal' self (amazed at the dream he assumes he's been having); Philostrate is ordered to turn "melancholy forth to funerals" in order to awaken "the pert and nimble spirit of mirth"; Hermia is threatened with drastic trans-formation (death or the "livery of a nun" or her father's choice of marriage partner); Egeus (a pre-echo of Brabantio in *Othello*) claims his daughter has been transformed from obedience by witchcraft to a "stubborn harshness"; Helena turns into a traitor, thinks of herself as a spaniel; the relationship of Oberon and Titania is transformed by jealousy and, in consequence, nature too has suffered a drastic global change; love changes the complexion of filial duty and friendship; Titania is cruelly changed to, and then from, a state of infatuation; she herself promises to purge Bottom's "mortal grossness" and turn him into an "airy spirit"; Thisbe is killed by a lion and Bottom kills himself and both come back to life to take their bows. Finally we may say the play transforms actors into parts and that the audience is transformed from a normal pre-play waking state to immersion in the dream-that-is-the-play to be finally reawakened by its own applause. At base, *A Midsummer Night's Dream* is about the transformative power of love. It is also about the transformative power of the imagination. The play is a series of interlinking patterns of metamorphosis.

Ovid is responsible for supplying the name Titania (an epithet, denoting status as a Titan, given to Artemis/Diana the Moon Goddess), as well as the story of Pyramus and Thisbe, and partly perhaps for the suggestion of Bottom's ass-head in the story of Midas. The list of entertainments read out by Philostrate in Act V (each of them, by the way, dealing with *unhappy* endings) is of stories found in *Metamorphoses*.

Francis Meres, quoted above, likening Shakespeare to Ovid, was, strictly speaking, referring to the poems, 'Venus and Adonis', 'The Rape of Lucrece' and what he called Shakespeare's "sugared Sonnets among his private friends". It is, however, for all to see that the witty soul of Ovid is also alive in *A Midsummer Night's Dream* … as it is

later in *The Tempest*, with which our play shares common features –
correspondences between Puck and Ariel, Oberon and Prospero,
Bottom and Caliban – both plays dealing with the theme of
redemption through love.

Notes

1 It is evident in Lysander's:

> For aught that I could ever read,
> Could ever hear by tale or history,
> The course of true love never did run smooth.
>
> (Act 1, scene 1, 132-4)

Hermia, in lines 168 to 178, is surely relying on things she's read when she
discourses on Cupid, Venus, and Dido and Aeneas. One would expect lovers
to know Petrarch's poetry and the essential guidebook to courtly behaviour
and love, Castiglione's *The Courtier* translated into English in 1561.

3

Midsummer Madness

This time the chapter heading is taken from another play, *Twelfth Night*. Olivia's reaction to the hilarious spectacle of Malvolio in yellow, cross-gartered stockings inanely smiling is "Why, this is very midsummer madness." A footnote will tell you midsummer is a time "traditionally associated with irresponsible and eccentric behaviour" (Wells) ... like the celebrations of Twelfth Night itself when Misrule is given licence. In both plays connection with the rites and customs of Twelfth Night and Midsummer – both festivals (winter and summer solstices) in ways being similar – give the plays permission to show the world turned topsy-turvy.

We are tapping into something deeply pagan (sub-Christian) and folkloric but let's remember as we do so that what are to us now superstitions were once beliefs. The summer solstice is 21st June, the longest day in the calendar when the sun reaches its zenith; Midsummer's Eve, however, is 23rd June – the Christian Church having moved Midsummer (the summer solstice) to 24th June, declaring it to be the feast day of St John the Baptist, thus making it a counterpart to the feast day six months earlier of Christ on 24th December. Men with the name of John or its equivalent (Jan, Johannes, Hans, etc.) had important parts to play on 24th June. This Christianising of a pagan occasion seems to have had little effect: pre-Christian observances and rituals energetically continued. It is a time ordinary folk welcomed summer. Midsummer in many countries was, and still is, a festival of bonfires. What is being celebrated and venerated is the metamorphic movement from the darkness of winter to the life-bringing light and warmth of summer. Midsummer is the day the fiery sun conquers night and darkness. (Light has long been considered, in intellectual quarters, a symbol of civilised life). For druids Midsummer signified the marriage of Heaven and Earth.

Midsummer's Eve, the shortest night in the year, was a time of fire festivals – fire the most transformative of the elements. It is a time for weeding and the burning of weeds, a time of love magic, oracles; the time spirits and demons were banished; the evil of witches circumvented; when maidens could discover who their future husbands might be; when wells and springs were venerated; flowers and herbs with healing properties picked at this special time were valued; health and fertility were uppermost in people's minds; dew collected on Midsummer morning had healing power. (We will see later, when we come to consider the story of Diana and Acteon, how the Moon goddess, seen bathing naked, sprinkled Acteon with water and by this means turned him into a stag). It was thought that if you spent Midsummer's Eve at a sacred site you might have the gift of poetry bestowed upon you; you might also just end up mad, dead, or carried off by the fairies. As we can already see, some of these things are woven into the fabric of *A Midsummer Night's Dream* and provide it with motifs and meaning[1]. The entered wood is a place of magic, of danger, of transformations; it is equivalent to the heroic journeys to the underworld that are found in many mythologies. To psychologists the wood represents the subconscious. (Remember that Demetrius complains that he's "wood" (mad) "within this wood".) Jung for instance tells us:

> the forest dark and impenetrable to the eye, like deep water and the sea, is the container of the unknown and the mysterious. It is an appropriate synonym for the unconscious. Trees, like fishes in water, represent the living contents of the unconscious … the mighty old oak represents a central figure among the contents of the unconscious, possessing personality in the most marked degree. It is a prototype of the Self, a symbol of the source and the goal of the individuation process. The oak stands for the still unconscious core of the personality, the plant symbolism indicating a state of deep uncon-sciousness. From this it may be concluded that the hero of fairytale is profoundly unconscious of himself. He is one of the 'sleepers', the 'blind' or 'blind-folded'.

Without going into this deeply, let's simply note that the oak in *A Midsummer Night's Dream* is associated with Theseus: Quince tells the mechanicals "At the Duke's oak we meet" – (the Oak King in folklore was said to be the god of the waxing year, the Holly King the god of the waning year). The play has much to do with sleeping (perchance to dream) and waking; and a theme of blindness runs through it, made obvious in references to Cupid:

> Love looks not with the eyes, but with the mind,
> And therefore is winged Cupid painted blind.
>> (Act I, scene 1, 234-5)

Of course, ironically, romantic comedy stresses the reverse, as we have noted – love looking *with* the eyes – is also true. Comedy thrives on error, complication, paradox, and mistaken identity.

Dr Johnson said, "I know not why Shakespeare calls this play a Midsummer Night's Dream, when he so carefully informs us that it happened on the night preceding *May* day." His puzzlement comes from Theseus, in Act IV, saying the lovers "rose up early to observe/ The rite of May". But 'Maying', as Stanley Wells points out, was "not confined to 1 May; it could happen at various times." Theseus confuses matters by alluding to February with his statement to the waking lovers in Act IV that "Saint Valentine is past". The title, then, like that of *Twelfth Night*, is not to be treated as definitive. It has something of the mock self-deprecation we find in titles like *Much Ado About Nothing*, *As You Like It* or *Twelfth Night's* subtitle *What You Will*. It is, of course, a dream we are entering and in dreams anything is possible, time is suspended and place becomes fluid. As suggested earlier, the title provides Shakespeare with licence to show the world turned upside down, as well as tapping us into a folkloric world of potent rituals (Maying, St Valentine's Day and the rites of the Moon are all referred to), a world of magically metamorphic happenings. The title is descriptive not definitive.

It has led to speculations that the play was commissioned for a specific occasion, one on which noble marriage/marriages might have been celebrated. It opens with expectation of marriage and by the start of Act V three marriages have taken place, and a further marriage (Oberon and Titania) has been restored to amity, and blessings for an ensuing fertility (sprinkled with "field-dew consecrate") bestowed.

Tempting though this is – and many commentators are attracted to the idea – there is no evidence for such a commission or performance. A.L. Rowse for instance is convinced the play was written to celebrate the marriage of the mother of Shakespeare's patron, the Earl of Southampton, to Sir Thomas Heneage, the Queen's Vice-Chamberlain, on 2nd May 1594. Maureen Duffy suggests it may have been written "for that same double wedding at Essex House in November 1596 for which Spenser wrote his *Prothalamium*"² and goes as far as to interpret it as an elaborate allegory in which Diana is Elizabeth and Essex is Acteon. (It is certainly true that the reference to the "fair vestal thronèd in the west" is to the Queen, and her pensioners are alluded to, but it doesn't follow that the Queen was present during performance). These speculations may be good sport but it is better to see the play's ending in marriage or multiple marriages as primarily a convention of romantic comedy.

An important aspect of pagan or folk belief is the idea that the universe is animate, a living entity, imbued with spirits and presided over by deities, their role generally protective but who must be propitiated if the protection is to be sustained, if the sun is to rise again in the morning and the moon appear in the night. They are not passive; their role is to activate nature; they have powers to change things. And these powers have their ambivalences: spirits and deities can play tricks, curse or bless, behave immorally, amorally, unpredictably; they can reward and punish – people, nymphs, animals can be pursued and turned into other things. Logic is totally suspended. The immortals in the play, like the classical gods, are capricious. Puck seems amoral: he describes his behaviour for either good or ill in equal terms; his jests simply make Oberon smile; he makes mistakes and blames fate for them; he has no high opinion of mortal beings. In other words we can legitimately view the magic in the wood and the behaviour of the immortals as ambivalent: the row between Oberon and Titania has caused universal havoc; she has no qualms about ordering her fairies to remove the legs from bees and the wings of butterflies; she imperiously tells Bottom "Thou wilt remain here, whether thou wilt or no". It is this animate dimension filled with airy spirits that *A Midsummer Night's Dream* taps into; it is clearly a world in which power can be exercised for good or evil. At the end of the play Puck promises safeguards against birth defects.

What is left unsaid is what causes these.

What animates human beings is the soul, the changeless inhabitant of the change-fraught body. The Christian equivalent to the fairies as activating spirits is angels and devils able to travel between the heavenly or hellish regions and the sublunary world of man and nature.

Notes

[1] Some of these country beliefs and customs were still alive in the novels of Thomas Hardy. See, especially, *The Woodlanders*.

[2] "Prothalamium or a spousall verse made by Edm. Spencer in honour of the double marriage of the two honourable and vertuous ladies, the Ladie Elizabeth, and the Ladie Katherine Somerset, daughters to the Right Honourable the earle of Worcester, and espoused to the two worthie gentlemen M. Henry Gilford, and M. William Peter, Esquires." This was published in 1596.

4

And Then The Moon

I feel sure that, when he was writing his 'Ode to a Nightingale', Keats' mind was alive with memories of *A Midsummer Night's Dream*. His word "darkling" ("Darkling I listen") appears in Act II in Helena's plea to Demetrius: "O, wilt thou darkling leave me? Do not so!" His Athenian wood is the garden of his Hampstead friend, Charles Brown, with its famous plum tree, under which, "darkling", Keats listened to the song of a nightingale, his "light-wingèd Dryad of the trees." The night is tender and:

> ... haply the Queen-Moon is on her throne,
> Clustered around by all her starry fays.

The nightingale we know from Ovid was once Philomela, daughter of King Pandion of Athens, raped by King Tereus and turned into a bird (the "inviolable voice" of Eliot's *The Waste Land*). What Keats is doing is contemplating a vision of immortality ("Thou wast not born for death, immortal Bird!"), trying to see his nightingale (like Yeats' "Miracle, bird or golden handiwork" in 'Sailing to Byzantium') as an emblem of eternity, of the soul we mentioned earlier and/or of the enduring power of art. He cannot see the bird singing in the plum tree but he can hear its inviolable voice. In the process, as in *A Midsummer Night's Dream*, other senses are consequently heightened. As Hermia tells us:

> Dark night that from the eye his function takes
> The ear more quick of apprehension makes.

Wherein it doth impair the seeing sense
It pays the hearing double recompense.

(Act III, scene 2, 177-80)

As well as this double recompense of hearing, Keats is also overwhelmed by the sweet odours of flowers ("I cannot see what flowers are at my feet ... but in embalmèd darkness guess each sweet") – and flowers ("of odious savours sweet"), as we know, have an important role in our play.

In the fairies' song of Act II of *A Midsummer Night's Dream*, Philomel is invited to act as a protective spirit and sing in a "sweet lullaby" designed to ease Titania into sleep. I am reminded of Coleridge's beautiful lines in 'The Ancient Mariner' in which the Moon is metamorphosed into the Virgin Mary:

Oh sleep! It is a gentle thing,
Beloved from pole to pole!
To Mary Queen the praise be given!
She sent the gentle sleep from Heaven,
That slid into my soul.

(The word "slid" here is one of my personal moments of *frisson*, an absolute word absolutely placed).

Keats' poem remembers "magic casements, opening on the foam/ Of perilous seas, in faery lands forlorn". And it is this last word "forlorn" that provokes the questions:

Was it a vision, or a waking dream?
Fled is that music – Do I wake or sleep?

... exactly the questions asked by the play.

A Midsummer Night's Dream is Queen-Moon-dominated: she presides over the action of the play, as Elizabeth I presided over the affairs of England. Shakespeare and his audience were well aware of the Moon's place in classical mythology. To the Greeks she was Selene then later Artemis, daughter of Hyperion and Thea, and sister of the sun god, Helios; to the Romans she was Luna or Diana, sister to the sun god, Phoebus Apollo (Bottom's "Phibbus" in the play's second scene). She was also known as Phoebe (meaning pure, bright) and Cynthia. (Elizabeth I was frequently addressed by these names

... and she is, as we have said, complimented in the play). Diana is protective of the night, of sleep and dreams; the goddess of women and childbirth, of hunting and wild nature; the sudden deaths of women were attributed to her arrows. If the male principle of Phoebus Apollo (also associated with archery, prophecy, as well as music) drove across the sky in a golden chariot, she, the female principle, drove across it in a silver one; a virgin, fleet of foot, she walked and danced in silver sandals (Walter De la Mare has the beautiful lines "Slowly, silently, now the moon/Walks the night in her silver shoon"); she also offers protection to wild beasts and young children. One of her metamorphic guises is Titania – Diana was a Titan-born goddess. Selene/Artemis eventually becomes associated with Hecate, goddess of the dark side of the moon, of nights the moon cannot be seen, and therefore of witchcraft. It was thought that Selene governed the sky, Artemis (as the new moon) the earth, and Hecate the lower world. One may remember Orlando's lines in *As You Like It*:

> ... thou, thrice-crowned queen of night, survey
> With thy chaste eye, from thy pale sphere above,
> Thy huntress' name that my full life doth sway.
>
> (Act III, scene 2, 1-3)

A waxing moon, because it increased in size, was thought to be pregnant with life; the waning moon, moving into darkness, was associated with magic and the power to heal and transform but also to destroy.

Two particular stories concerning Diana are of relevance, one of which we have already mentioned – the story, found in Ovid, of her encounter with Acteon. Diana (Artemis) the huntress was bathing naked with her nymphs in a pool when Acteon, out hunting, inadvertently appeared; she splashed him with water, which transformed him into a deer or stag, whereupon, horrifyingly retaining his human consciousness, he was torn to pieces by his own hounds. Some accounts provide motives: that Zeus was angry with him for wooing Semele, whom Zeus himself desired; another was that he angered the Moon-Goddess in claiming he was a better hunter than she was or by wanting to marry her. The most familiar story is the one given in Ovid. Not only was Acteon humanly conscious of his horrible fate, his companions urged the hounds on, while at the same time looking about for their friend. A comic parallel to this in the play would be that of Bottom's companions confronted with an ass-head. Additionally, one can't help being reminded of Orsino's lines in *Twelfth Night*:

> O, when mine eyes did see Olivia first ...
> That instant was I turned into a hart,
> And my desires, like fell and cruel hounds,
> E'er since pursue me.
>
> (Act I, scene 1, 20-4)

The other story is of Endymion (the subject of a long poem by Keats). Because of Endymion's beauty, the Moon-Goddess (Selene) fell in love with him and provided him with 50 daughters. An outraged Zeus allowed him to pass sentence on himself: Endymion chose everlasting sleep in a cave on Mount Latmus, with the provision he remain forever young. The Moon (Selene/Diana/Phoebe/Luna/Cynthia) visited him every night, in some stories simply to gaze on or kiss him, in others to wake him for love-making. The kissing is a pleasing metaphor for moonlight falling upon the earth. Again, parallels to events in *A Midsummer Night's Dream*, in which a good deal of sleeping/dreaming takes place, are clear.

It is likely that Shakespeare knew the play *Endymion, the Man in the Moon*, a comedy written in prose by John Lyly in 1588 and printed in 1591. It is interesting to note that Lyly's play ends with a tribute to Elizabeth I and has variously been interpreted as a political allegory concerning the Queen and the Earl of Leicester. Those who wish to understand *A Midsummer Night's Dream* in these terms (see Maureen Duffy) – and it is not altogether implausible – usually cite Lyly's play as supporting evidence. Equating Diana and the Queen was a commonplace of the time. Duffy quotes a psalm-like poem by Sir Walter Raleigh printed in 1593 as an instance that makes it plain:

> Praised be Diana's fair and harmless light
> Praised be the dews, wherewith she moists the ground;
> Praised be her beams, the glory of the night
> Praised be her power, by which her powers abound.
> Praised be her nymphs, with whom she decks the woods,
> Praised be her knights, in whom true honour lives,

Praised be that force, by which she moves the floods;
Let that Diana shine, which all these gives.

In heaven Queen she is among the spheres;
In aye she Mistress like makes all things pure
Eternity in her oft change she bears;
She beauty is, by her the fair endure.

But, as already stated, the evidence for treating the play as an allegory involving particular persons of the time is circumstantial.

A final note: in Marian iconography Diana becomes the Virgin Mary sometimes portrayed standing on a crescent moon.

5

By Moonlight

The moon determines the ebb and flow of tides and the precipitation of dew; she shines a light in darkness; and, like the menstrual cycle, she renews herself each month. She is also a wanderer. Oberon tells Titania "We the globe can compass soon,/Swifter than the wandering moon". It is said that sleeping exposed to the moon's rays caused people to go mad and sleeping under the light of a full moon caused women to become pregnant.

When the play opens we are between a waning and a waxing moon. We find Theseus impatient with the moon's progress (it's another four days to the wedding ceremony):

> ... Four happy days bring in
> Another moon – but O, methinks how slow
> This old moon wanes! She lingers my desires,
> Like to a stepdame or a dowager
> Long withering out a young man's revenue.
>
> (Act I, scene 1, 2-6)

He is in two minds: the "nuptial hour" draws on "apace" (will soon be here) but not quickly enough for his "desires". In other words he is sexually eager. She, however, comforts him with:

> Four days will quickly steep themselves in night;
> Four nights will quickly dream away the time:
> And then the moon – like to a silver bow
> New-bent in heaven – shall behold the night
> Of our solemnities.
>
> (Act I, scene 1, 7-11)

What we need to understand here is that, despite what is said later about earlier promiscuities, Theseus and Hippolyta are observing the proper rites, remaining chaste (and the word "chaste" in reference to the moon comes up repeatedly) until their wedding night. His impatience is thus a compliment to her and her reassurance is a compliment to him. Theseus is to re-utter this only-human impatience later, when, with still three hours to go to bedtime, he asks:

> Come now, what masques, what dances shall we have
> To wear away this long age of three hours
> Between our after-supper and bedtime?
> Where is our usual manager of mirth?
> What revels are in hand? Is there no play
> To ease the anguish of a torturing hour?
>
> (Act V, scene 1, 33-8)

... "this long age" and "torturing hour" speak of sexual impatience ... though perhaps they might simply be read as an expression of a desire to make things ceremonially final and perfect, a consummation devoutly wished. But the main point is that these two mature lovers, despite his impatience, have got things under control in that they observe due ceremony. "The sealing day betwixt" Theseus and Hippolyta is fixed so as to create an "everlasting bond of fellowship". This is a case where love does indeed transpose to dignity and gives us the benchmark for judging those love-relationships that don't. There is only one aspiration higher than that of marriage and that is the absolute chastity of the religious devotee: "Thrice blessèd they that master so their blood." But Theseus, as we learn, has no warm feelings towards that sentiment!

Notice in Hippolyta's lines the notion that dreams are quickly over and time can be *made* to pass quickly. Time is perceived differently by different characters. For some it moves quickly; for some it drags. The fairies are all allegro: Titania tells them in Act II, "Come, now a roundel and a fairy song,/Then for the third part of an minute hence." Lysander is aware of transience, the quickness of time ("Swift as a shadow, short as any dream"); Helena is lento: in tones worthy of Bottom's Pyramus, she declares in Act III, "O weary night! O long and tedious night."

A Midsummer Night's Dream is a play of meetings and of lovers' trysts. The next time we hear of the moon is in Egeus' accusation that Lysander has bewitched his daughter, Hermia, by singing "by moonlight at her window". This is the Hecate moon, a moon of dark and secret deceptions (the word "feigning" is used twice – a word often used, incidentally, to describe the composition of poetry). Hermia's crime is disobedience and for this she stands to pay the penalty with her life. It is the law of Athens and Theseus is its embodiment. He offers Hermia a choice either of obedience to her father or to become a nun:

> ... a barren sister all your life,
> Chanting faint hymns to the cold fruitless moon.
>
> (Act I, scene 1, 72-3)

This view of the moon as cold and fruitless runs counter to the positive values earlier ascribed to it. In his mouth, the words reinforce the severity of the law but also betray something of the impatience with the moon we have already noted. To worship at Diana's altar means "to protest/For aye austerity and single life", to end up a bit like Lysander's widow aunt ("she hath no child") – in other words quite opposite to Theseus' immediate expectations. He makes chastity sound as disagreeable as death, if not as a kind of death itself (certain ironies come into play if we remember the Elizabethan's punning habit with the sexual meaning of 'to die'). But perhaps he is simply trying to get Hermia to focus her mind, giving her till the "next new moon" to make her decision. The moon in this opening scene therefore is playing an active and decisive role – quite different from, say, the moon in Eliot's 'Rhapsody on a Windy Night', who, like an old courtesan:

> ... winks a feeble eye,
> She smiles into corners.
> She smoothes the hair of the grass.
> The moon has lost her memory.
> A washed-out smallpox cracks her face,
> Her hand twists a paper rose,
> That smells of dust and eau de Cologne,
> She is alone
> With all the old nocturnal smells
> That cross and cross across her brain.

Left alone, Lysander and Hermia plot an escape that takes them into the wood and the dark night. He has a premonition of what might happen there, when he talks of how "quick bright things come to confusion" ... quick (meaning alive) and bright reminding us that Phoebe's name translates as pure, bright. He is imagining the moon to be actively on the side of lovers, making it therefore an accomplice to dark deeds. He is to say to Helena, who now comes in to make a threesome:

> Tomorrow night, when Phoebe doth behold
> Her silver visage in the watery glass,
> Decking with liquid pearl the bladed grass –
> A time that lovers' flights doth still conceal –
> Through Athens gates have we devised to steal.
>
> (Act I, scene 1, 209-13)

He is unaware of implied dangers. Acteon saw Diana naked, doubtless enjoying her reflection in the fatal pool. There is also a suggestion of something narcissistic, self-regarding, as well as the possibility of lovers becoming mad (*luna*cy) in forgetting themselves in their infatuation or state of enchantment. The dew is both the water sprinkled on Acteon and a symbol of fertility nourishing the grass. Again ambivalence provides the play with motive power.

Unfortunate meetings are associated with moonlight. The mechanicals, seeking seclusion for the rehearsing of their play (and not getting it), are meant to meet at the Duke's oak by moonlight; Titania and Oberon are cursedly "ill-met by moonlight"; the lovers blunder about beneath the "chaste beams of the watery moon"; Pyramus and Thisbe meet by moonlight. (There is a point of contrast in Theseus' words "Fair lovers you are fortunately met" – that event taking place in daylight).

The fairies associate the moon with swiftness and with dewing "her orbs upon the green". If night is the time for sleeping together under a guardian moon, then the dissension between Titania and Oberon has caused her to forswear his bed. The result is catastrophic: the moon as "the governess of floods" has been provoked into making the winds suck up from the sea:

> Contagious fogs which, falling in the land,
> Hath every pelting river made so proud
> That they have overborne their continents.
>
> (Act II, scene 1, 90-2)

and

> Pale in her anger, washes all the air,
> That rheumatic diseases do abound.
>
> (Act II, scene 1, 104-5)

Chaos is come again. This is a vengeful moon turning everything to a state of unhealthy disorder. (The transgression of the thin line between order and disorder is a constant theme of Shakespeare's plays and it is sometimes said that the Elizabethans were fearfully obsessed by a vision of impending chaos). Titania and Oberon, as guardians of nature, have, by their jealousy, incurred the wrath of Diana. The punishment has global consequences. A curse is on the land. We are meant to be attending a wedding and blessing it. In tune with the ships whose "sails conceive/And grow big-bellied with the wanton wind" which Titania and her votaress, looking out to sea, once watched, and nature itself, our married couples are supposed to be blessed with fertility. Here again is that ambivalence that energises the play so effectively. And while we are mentioning curses, let's remind ourselves that oaths, curses, spells, charms were, at this time, taken seriously.

Commentators usually point to the fact that Elizabethan England was experiencing a series of bad summers. But this has faint importance compared to the way Shakespeare is using Titania's famous speech to underscore the theme of fertility that runs through the play. What we need to register is that the moon isn't always a benign influence; that failure to propitiate her can lead to dire consequences; that life-giving liquids can be metamorphosed into damaging mists and floods.

Refusing to join the fairies' "moonlight revels", Oberon, like Theseus, thinks in terms of a "cold moon" and remembers seeing Cupid journeying between the moon and the earth and failing to strike a "fair vestal thronèd in the west" ... an "imperial votaress" with his "fiery shaft" – the reference to Elizabeth I, who, mythologised as the Virgin Queen, remained 'fancy-free' (i.e. untouched by sensual love). Note that Cupid can miss.

Later in the play Oberon, the king of shadows, will cause the moon to be hidden in mist, telling Puck to:

> ... overcast the night.
> The starry welkin cover thou anon
> With drooping fog as black as Acheron.

(Act III, scene 2, 355-7)

... a parallel to the actions of the governess of floods as reported by Titania in Act II cannot be avoided.

Cupid (Eros to the Greeks) was a god of sexual love, closely connected with Venus (Aphrodite to the Greeks). She is the goddess of beauty and sensual love and has her presence in the sky as the morning or evening star. She too can punish, especially when love is met with rejection. In Act III Demetrius points to her: "yonder Venus in her glimmering sphere". (This star is also ambivalently known as Lucifer, the light-bearer, Satan). The early Greeks worshipped Eros as a beautiful winged youth but later saw him as mischievous, carrying a flaming torch to kindle the passion of lovers or a bow and arrows – again the theme of hunting – the arrows being of two kinds: sharp ones with golden tips to wound with love and blunt ones with lead tips to repulse it. Puck is a metamorphosis of Cupid; we can see obvious parallels: the mischief, the promotion of love-hate tensions between the lovers, the connection with the flower maidens call love-in-idleness (the pansy), once white but transformed by Cupid's shaft to the purple of "love's wound". This flower, with its power to make "man or woman madly dote", may be said to stand in for Cupid's torch. The sexual symbolism in all this is obvious. As is the quenching of Cupid's arrow in the "chaste beams of the watery moon".

For the moment, however, let's simply register the connections between flowers, arrows, moon, water (metamorphosed into the juice of the flower), eyes (which can water and into which juice is placed), sleep, seeing and blindness (Cupid is blind), mischief and love.

Titania's moon is determined by her infatuation for Bottom. She has him awakened by asking her fairies to "fan the moonbeams from his sleeping eyes". At first hearing one might think she is making the suggestion that the moon is anti-chastity and therefore on the side of sexual pleasure:

> The moon methinks looks with a watery eye;
> And when she weeps, weeps every little flower,
> Lamenting some enforcèd chastity.
>
> (Act III, scene 1, 193-5)

It is more likely that the word "enforced" here means quite the opposite ... not forced into being chaste but being sexually violated, the fate of Philomela, the chastity awaiting Hermia. Again we notice the connection between the moon, watery weeping, and dew-bedecked flowers.

The mechanicals' moon constitutes a gross parody. Pyramus and Thisbe parallel Oberon and Titania in that they too "meet by moonlight" but their moon isn't classically derived: its source is folkloric and, according to Stanley Wells, biblical – it is masculine, with a bush of thorns, a dog and a lantern. Wells tells us that he is "the man who picked up sticks on the Sabbath day" as recorded in *Numbers 15. 32-6* ... where the man in question, on the orders of God and Moses, was stoned to death for doing so. In some retellings of the story the man is banished to the moon. We may be reminded of lines in *The Tempest* in which the "mooncalf", Caliban, admiringly asks Stephano:

> Caliban: Hast thou not dropped from heaven?
>
> Stephano: Out o' th' moon, I do assure thee. I was the Man
>   i' th' moon when time was.
>
> Caliban: I have seen thee in her, and I do adore thee. My
>   mistress showed me thee, and thy dog, and thy
>   bush.
>
> (Act II, scene 2, 142-7)

The moon of Bottom and his crew is both folkloric (there are well-known nursery rhymes about it) and comically literal: the would-be actors consult a calendar to see if a 'real' moon is shining on the night of the nuptials and feel need to have its light either enter through a casement or have to "present the person of moonshine". They opt for the latter. The contrast with Diana/Titania/Elizabeth could not be greater. In context, their moon is absurd. Starveling plays the part laconically: it may be that stage nerves make him want to get his part over as quickly as possible or that he is literal-minded and delivers deadpan; but perhaps too he, more heroically, loses patience with the cynics in the audience.

In line with the confusion of the senses that takes place in *A Midsummer Night's Dream*, we are asked, during the *lamentable comedy*, to "listen to the moon". Demetrius turns the adjective hornèd, applied to the moon, into a joke about cuckoldry to which the rational Theseus replies: "He is no crescent, and his horns are invisible within the circumference". One can either take this as a continuation of the joke or perhaps as a rebuke that Demetrius should pay more respect. The courtly audience's comments in this scene are mostly ambiguous. Hippolyta, for instance, in contrast with her sentiments at the beginning of the play, declares herself "aweary of this moon. Would he would change". This is either an expression of boredom or an indication that she, like Theseus, is impatient for bedtime. Now the roles are reversed: it is he who urges patience and good manners with the words "But yet in courtesy, in all reason, we must stay the time". She will, in a minute, applaud with "Well shone, Moon! Truly, the moon shines with a good grace", the word "grace" having religious overtones. Whether this is spoken with irony must depend on the production values of a particular staging. With the entrance of Bottom/Pyramus, the moon, after being thanked for its "sunny beams", is now associated with death: "Moonshine and Lion are left to bury the dead". The play's penultimate reference to the moon is Hippolyta's "How chance Moonshine is gone before Thisbe comes back and finds her lover?" to which her husband replies, "She will find him by starlight. Here she comes; and her passion ends the play."

Finally, as in *Cinderella*, the decisive "iron-tongue of midnight" sounds, the married couples go off to celebrate their marriage rites, Titania metamorphoses into Hecate in Puck's "the wolf behowls the moon" and in:

> Now the wasted brands do glow
> Whilst the screech-owl, screeching loud,
> Puts the wretch that lies in woe
> In remembrance of a shroud.
> Now it is the time of night

> That the graves, all gaping wide,
> Every one lets forth his sprite
>   In the churchway paths to glide.
> And we fairies, that do run
>   By the triple Hecate's team,
> From the presence of the sun
>   Following darkness like a dream,
> Now are frolic.

(Act V, scene 1, 365-77)

Theseus' palace is left in a post-coital "glimmering light" as fires turn to embers and die. After that, as in 'The Ancient Mariner', we may suppose:

> The moving Moon went up the sky,
> And nowhere did abide.

… though I am reminded of a Tony Hancock programme in which Hancock tells Sid James he wishes his house in Railway Cuttings had once had a famous occupant. In the night James loosens the wallpaper and pencils verses on the wall. Next morning, discovering these, Hancock triumphantly recognises as the work of Byron the following:

> O Moon, thou art fair, O Moon thou art bright!
> Coming out again tomorrow night?

6

Eye Enthrallèd

It is tempting to see *A Midsummer Night's Dream* as a beautiful and highly-elaborate Renaissance tapestry, formally patterned, intricately woven, subtly textured, full of glowing colours. The drawback to the analogy is its one-dimensionality, its absence of sound and movement – what Keats was conscious of when he contemplated the Grecian urn. The idea of threads, however, is useful: following particular ones helps to add layers to our appreciation, deepen our experience. That said, it is never easy detaching things from other qualities and features with which they invariably have intimate connections without giving the impression of simplifying. We have so far said that this is a play of transformations, a play of meetings, and we have given a deal of consideration to the presiding influence of the moon. One thing I hope has become apparent is that within the play significances lie in the eyes of the beholders; characters each have different perceptions, see what they want to see; some of them also have their perceptions altered and involuntarily see what they are made to see. As we have noted, they each have different notions concerning the moon, ones that suit their purposes. It is not inaccurate therefore to see *A Midsummer Night's Dream* as a play of perceptions, of ways of seeing, being seen and not seen. Light and darkness play important parts. Blind Cupid, Puck, Oberon involve themselves in changing perceptions: lovers, meant to see "not with the eye but with the mind", do exactly the opposite and therefore become subject to a form of comic madness; characters fall asleep and dream ("in such sleep what dreams may come?" asked Hamlet); there is an interplay of shadows and visions; Oberon and Puck have the power of invisibility and so an interplay of seeing and not-seeing, hearing but not seeing, keeps occurring. These all interconnect with the patterns of metamorphosis and with lunar influence. We have already noticed that the action of the play moves from day to night and back again to daylight and through altered forms of consciousness – as well as physically altered form, as in the case of Bottom and his troupe, members of which become a wall, a man-in-the-moon, a lion etc. In the darkness of the wood, seeing is made possible by the active presence of moonshine – the moon has eyes to see and shed tears with – but the wood is also a place of distorted vision, of *luna*cy, and a place where seeing is tampered with.

By now we know that in a romantic comedy love looking through the eyes is the start of trouble. In *Love's Labours Lost* Berowne in his paean to love tells us "A lover's eyes will gaze an eagle blind". Theseus mockingly says the lover sees "Helen's beauty in a brow of Egypt" (which some commentators interpret as signifying gypsy, others as 'black-skinned'). One consequence of this, as wisely declared by Bottom, is that "the truth, reason, and love keep little company". We need to remind ourselves that reason is important as a guiding principle in Elizabethan affairs: without it one could not hope to achieve the good life, a life based upon the avoidance of extremes and excess, the so-called Golden Mean formulated by the Greeks. The body-politic, according to Sir Thomas Elyot in his *Boke named the Governour* (1531) was "disposed by the order of equity, and governed by the rule and moderation of reason". "Temperance", in the words of Thomas Wilson (*The Arte of Rhetorique*, 1553/1560) "is a measuring of affections according to the will of reason, and the subduing of lust unto the square of honesty". Reason is a major component of the "marriage of true minds" (see Shakespeare's sonnet 116 which begins "Let me not to the marriage of true minds/Admit impediments, love is not love/Which alters when it alteration finds"): lovers in romantic comedies are at first incapable of seeing things rationally but then hopefully, finally are brought round to that condition. One obvious opposite to reason is the unreason produced by allowing the senses too much licence – sight most particularly in the case of lovers. As Lysander says – ironically under the spell of the magic juice – to Helena:

The will of man is by his reason swayed,
And reason says you are the worthier maid.
Things growing are not ripe until their season;
So I, being young, till now ripe not to reason.
And touching now the point of human skill,
Reason becomes the marshal to my will,
And leads me to your eyes, where I o'erlook
Love's stories written in love's richest book.

(Act II, scene 2, 121-8)

He is perfectly right in what he says of reason (Donne calls reason "God's viceroy in me") though his mental condition undercuts what he says, the reference to eyes and the literary associations of the last line giving the game away.

When love comes in through the eye, reason goes out of the window. If, as Hooker (1547) says "Obedience of creatures unto the Law of Nature is the stay of the whole world" (the Law of Nature being God's hierarchically-ordained order of Creation), then Hermia's disobedience to her father is a serious legal matter. "I would my father looked but with my eyes," she tells the Duke, only to be rebuked with the words "Rather your eyes must with his judgement look". Shakespeare's plays frequently deal with this dilemma – conflict between parent and offspring. One immediately thinks of Ophelia, Cordelia, Desdemona. Hermia is in the wrong and Egeus has right and the severity of the law on his side. His appeal to the Duke is just – even if he is, by the sound of it, aiming at a marriage of properties, suggested by his words "I do estate unto Demetrius", regardless of the fact it is generally known Demetrius has been courting Helena. The escape into the wood with Lysander compounds Hermia's disobedience. The thin line between comedy and tragedy is being walked. Hermia's unreason causes her to use hyperbolic language – a feature of infatuated lovers. She talks of the "tempest" of her eyes and complains of the unfairness of having to "choose love by another's eyes". Her eyes have 'chosen' Lysander (though Egeus maintains she has been bewitched); they have also attracted Demetrius, making Helena jealous: he is "doting on Hermia's eyes" which she has already described as "lodestars" (i.e. the most attractive stars in the heavens). In fact, before "Demetrius looked on Hermia's eyne/He hailed down oaths that he was only mine." Jonathan Miller's

BBC production of 1981 had the nice touch of presenting a short-sighted Helena wearing spectacles.

Her statement that "Love looks not with the eyes, but with the mind" and the conviction it "can transpose to form and dignity" are important. They represent an ideal as opposed to the reality. In fact what Helena is saying is – to use the words of Orsino in *Twelfth Night* – "So full of shapes is fancy/That it alone is high fantastical". Wells' gloss on this is "love is prompted not by objective evidence of the senses, but by the fancies of the mind". In other words more like the seething brains of lovers and madmen that Theseus talks of. What she says is not therefore without irony. If love transposes to dignity, what do we say of her thinking of herself as a spaniel and asking to Demetrius to "spurn me, strike me/Neglect me, lose me"? Love has, in fact, debased her. It has interfered in and altered her friendship with Hermia. And the man she loves loves her friend. The green-eyed monster, jealousy has entered her life. She wishes she had Hermia's eyes – "For she hath blessèd and attractive eyes". So much for dignity! It destroys her ability to reason: she persuades herself she'll win Demetrius' affection by aiding him to pursue Hermia and Lysander into the wood:

> I will go tell him of fair Hermia's flight.
> Then to the wood will he tomorrow night
> Pursue her; and for this intelligence
> If I have thanks it is a dear expense.
> But herein mean I to enrich my pain,
> To have his sight thither, and back again.
>
> (Act I, scene 1, 246-51)

In addition to the fatally false logic of this, it is not too unjust to see a masochistic streak, a preparedness to be pathetic.

The lovers continually allude to sight/seeing/eyes – for example:

> Demetrius: Tempt not too much the hatred of my spirit;
> For I am sick when I do look on thee.
>
> Helena: And I am sick when I look not on you.
> (Act II, scene 1, 211-13)

And, of course, they are deprived of sight by sleep – though not of dreams: Hermia wakes crying

> Help me, Lysander, help me! Do thy best
> To pluck this crawling serpent from my breast!
> Ay me, for pity! – what a dream was here!
>
> (Act II, scene 2, 151-3)

The lovers' eyes are magically influenced – Titania's too. Her eye is "enthralled" to the "shape" of Bottom. Oberon makes connection between Cupid, the magic juice and eyes. In the case of Demetrius, we find him saying:

> Flower of this purple dye,
> Hit with Cupid's archery,
> Sink in apple of his eye.
> When his love he doth espy,
> Let her shine as gloriously
> As that Venus of the sky.
>
> (Act III, scene 2, 102-7)

They all continue, like Berowne, to find beauty in beloveds' eyes. Yet when they wake together on the morn of the nuptial ceremonies they wonder at what they see: Demetrius and Hermia, expressing amazement, state:

> Demetrius: These things seem small and indistinguishable,
> Like far-off mountains turnèd into clouds.
>
> Hermia: Methinks I see things with parted eye,
> When everything seems double.
>
> (Act IV, scene 1, 186-9)

Bottom – like Hermia, like Titania – wakes from a dream. And he too is seemingly transposed to indignity. Innocently caught up in the row between Oberon and Titania, he is unjustly debased to the level of a rough satyr … and yet in properly sympathetic productions he ironically retains his honest working-class dignity. (It is worth remembering that on Palm Sunday Christ rode into Jerusalem on a humble ass and that St Francis on his deathbed asked forgiveness of "my poor brother donkey", his body). He becomes an object in the perceptions of others and yet in my view doesn't become any more of an ass than his already-established character allows. In fact I would argue that he gains in dignity. His vice, if we may call it that, is an over-eagerness to please. He thinks his acting of Pyramus will provoke tears, advising the audience to "look to their eyes" (remember Blake's "Excess of sorrow laughs. Excess of joy weeps" and Philostrate's reaction, how the play in rehearsal made "mine eyes water; but more 'merry' tears/The passion of loud laughter never shed"). Bottom's innocence is confirmed in his reply to Snout's "What do I see on thee?" when he says "What do you see? You see an ass-head of your own, do you?" Later, in the role of Pyramus – and in keeping with the theme of the confusion of the senses that runs through the play – he says "I see a voice". It is not the first time he has ingenuously got things confused. I am convinced that Bottom's confusions – mostly to do with an undeterred lack of skill in handling language – are not to be interpreted as stupidity. Nor is his dream – as some directors would wish – a nightmare. He wakes from it with that innocent marvelling of Miranda in *The Tempest* catching sight of her brave new world. Bottom rubs his eyes and says:

> I have had a most rare vision. I have had a dream past the wit of man to say what dream it was. Man is but an ass if he go about to expound this dream. Methought I was – there is no man can tell what. Methought I was – and methought I had – but man is but a patched fool if he will offer to say what methought I had. The eye of man hath not heard, the ear of man hath not seen, man's hand is not able to taste, his tongue to conceive, nor his heart to report what my dream was! I will get Peter Quince to write a ballad of this dream. It shall be called 'Bottom's Dream', because it hath no bottom; and I will sing it in the latter end of a play before the Duke.
>
> (Act IV, scene 1, 203-14)

The ingenuousness of this (those three "methoughts") is made more certain by the fact that, unaware of it, Bottom is parodying words of St Paul to the Corinthians (1 Corinthians 2.9). Wells gives us the Bishop's Bible version in his notes:

The eye hath not seen, and the ear hath not heard, neither have entered into the heart of man, the things which God hath prepared for them that love him.

Eyes – and the qualities ascribed to them above – are consistently referred to and represent a distinctive thread – one among several – stitching the play together.

7

Wood Within This Wood

There is common consensus about Shakespeare's great skill in plotting the action of this play. Sometimes it is referred to as a "river plot" (I have even seen it described as being like a cake with four layers), in that it takes four storylines and has them flow into one another – or has them meet, that is, if, as we suggested earlier, *A Midsummer Night's Dream* is a play of meetings. Perhaps, however, it is truer to say that these storylines intrude into or collide with each other: the mortals intrude into and collide with the world of fairy, lose their way in it and are subjected to enchantments there. The fairies invite themselves into the world of the mortals – they have come from afar to bring blessings – though it really feels as though they belong as residents rather than visitors. This feeling comes from what is clearly a disparity between fairy time and 'real' time. A keynote of fairy existence is swiftness: Puck, remember, can girdle the earth in 40 minutes. It is as if fairy folk can be anywhere anytime. The 'mechanicals' – conveniently perhaps – go into the wood to rehearse. The rehearsal is aborted by Bottom's 'translation', which quickly scares Quince, Snug, Flute, Snout and Starveling out of it, leaving him to enjoy his beautiful dream. In a sense, the 'mechanicals' are out of place in the Athenian wood; it is not their milieu. It is worth noting that Quince refers to it as the "palace wood", clearly indicating it is in the ownership of Theseus as his hunting grounds. The presence of the fairies and the presiding influence of the moon indicate too that it has been magically metamorphosed. And while we are talking of intrusions, it may be pointed out that, during the performance of the lamentable comedy, the performers step outside of their roles and intrude into the world of the courtiers while at the same time the courtiers interrupt with intrusive comments.

And yet for all its sophisticated blending of various elements, *A Midsummer Night's Dream* is frequently thought of as a simple play – simpler, say, than *The Comedy of Errors*. Its plotting is so exact and seamless that it is usually taken for granted. One might get the impression from the way with which it is dealt in general commentaries or surveys that the play can take care of itself. This seeming ability to look after itself, plus its air of genial optimism and cheerfulness (the very qualities with which Bottom is endowed) is, in a cynical age, problematic. As long as seventy years ago, John Middleton Murry suggested we had become victims of a "fatal separation between the urban and the rustic mind", locating the beginnings of this separation in the "infliction of the Puritan Sabbath on the country-side under the Commonwealth". However that may be, Murry's observation that Shakespeare's high comedies are "saturated" with a sense of the open air is an accurate one. They require us to make an "effort of sympathetic imagination". Even if the "gulf" Murry talks about cannot, as he says, be wholly bridged, we have to see how far we can get by trying.

Another way of viewing the structure of the play is to see the main action in the wood framed by scenes set in Athens, with the return of the fairies as an epilogue. In a sense, Theseus and Hippolyta 'surround' the wood. We move from their civilised world, where they represent authority, into the wood, where normal behaviour is suspended, to be restored to civilised mores and behaviour in the final Act. In fact, it is Theseus and Hippolyta (the world of waking-consciousness belongs to them) who come to retrieve us and take us back, changed by the experience, to normality. It is the same pattern as going from being awake to falling asleep and then being re-awakened. Locating Shakespeare's comedies in "the tradition of the seasonal ritual play", Northrop Frye has this to say:

> We may call it the drama of the green world, its plot being assimilated to the ritual theme of the triumph of life and love over the waste land...The action of the comedy begins in a world represented as a normal world, moves into the green world, goes into a metamorphosis there in which the comic resolution is achieved, and returns to the normal world.

In each of these worlds, as in Eden, there are serpents. The play opens with the expectation of happy nuptials but the situation is suddenly confronted with a dilemma: we have unruly youngsters to deal with, threatening the celebrations. In the wood, things are even worse: the whole of the natural order has been turned inside out as a result, as we said earlier, of the Adam-and-Eve-like conflict between Oberon and Titania. The serpent jealousy is to blame. (In Marian iconography the Virgin Mary is sometimes portrayed with a serpent crushed beneath her feet).

So the play drags us through a seemingly dangerous wood and out back into the open – where we meet daylight, rubbing our eyes, now able to see things differently, ready to get married, and be entertained by faithful servants. It is like an initiation ceremony, a rite of passage into adulthood.

8

Filled Up With Mud

Nature, that fram'd us of four elements
Warring within our breasts for regiment.
Marlowe: Tamburlaine Part One

John Donne described Man as "a little world made cunningly of Elements, and an Angelic sprite". These "Elements" attach human beings to the earth; the "Angelic sprite" is the soul, which connects them with the angels and to eternity. The four elements are, of course, air, fire, earth and water. Everything on earth, according to general Elizabethan belief, rooted in Greek philosophy, is composed of the four elements in varying mixes. And the elements have their own spheres: the earth (we still call it that) on which man has his earthly life is at the centre of the universe; above it is the sphere of water (explained by the fact that rain descends on the earth); then air; and finally fire, beyond which comes the sphere of the moon. God is said to have especially positioned air to separate the opposing elements fire and water. They were ascribed qualities: earth, being the heaviest and the lowest, is cold and dry; water is cold and moist; air hot and moist; fire hot and dry. Air and fire ascend; earth and water go down. Elizabethan psychology (if we can call it that) was based on whatever element was dominant in a person's character. It was thought that there were four basic types: sanguine (air), choleric (fire), melancholic (earth), and phlegmatic (water). In the celestial regions above the moon, the elements were thought to be mixed equally and therefore incorruptible. As Donne puts it in his poem 'The Good-Morrow', "What ever dyes, was not mixed equally."

M.M. Reese tells us:

> The continuity of intellectual belief was yet undisturbed, for
> the Renaissance had accepted from the Middle Ages a vast
> bulk of ossified doctrine about man, a traditional amalgam of
> Christian with pagan philosophy.

Some knowledge of this is helpful. The action of *A Midsummer
Night's Dream*, as we have established, takes place beneath the gaze
of the moon, where, to quote Donne again:

> Dull sublunary lovers love
> (Whose soul is sense) cannot admit
> Absence, because it doth remove
> Those things that elemented it.
>> ('A Valediction': forbidding mourning)

The play concerns sublunary lovers and seems to me to be
predominantly watery. Jonathan Miller's production, mentioned
earlier, recognises this by having the lovers in the wood thrashing
about in moonlit pools, getting themselves in the process, from the
mix of water and earth, decidedly muddy. The play is full of liquids:
tears, dew, the juice of love-in-idleness, a watery moon, tides;
Hermia's cheeks are pale "belike for want of rain", which can be
supplied from the "tempest" of her eyes; fields are drowned; the
nine men's morris is filled up with mud. Water and air combine to
make mists and fogs; winds suck up water from the sea. Fire and
water are connected in the quenching of Cupid's "fiery shaft". We
are made aware of earth through growing things – trees, flowers,
beasts of the field – all needing the blessing of "dew consecrate"; a
wall of lime and loam appears; and the hard-handed mechanicals
are nearer to the earth (the salt of the earth!) than the refined courtly
ones ... though, as we have just suggested, they undergo, as part of
their rite of passage, a direct connection with it, having to rest
themselves on hard ground or become muddied like the nine men's
morris. We are also made aware of the element of air through flight:
Cupid flying between the moon and earth, Puck like the sputnik
putting a girdle round the earth in 40 minutes, flitting fairies
wandering swifter than the moon's sphere, arrows flying, birds,
insects, spirits; even the Moon flying through the night in her silver

chariot. Air too resonates with words (and through them colours enter the imagination), speeches, song and music, and breathes with odious savours sweet.

9

Very Tragical Mirth

A way of interpreting what goes on in a Shakespeare play is to consider how it is built up of patterns of opposites and to take note of how the tension between these energises the play into meaning. Drama, as we all know, thrives on conflict. Sometimes for comic effect opposites are mistaken for each other, as in Bottom's malapropisms and paradoxes. We have already mentioned the energising power of ambivalence ... which, we must admit, sometimes shades into ambiguity when Shakespeare leaves things open and unexplained, when he doesn't supply reasons or motives – so in a way guarding mystery ... it hath no bottom ... our play, after all, being concerned with magic and magical happenings. Magic, to state the obvious, is made *physically* present to us in the figures of Oberon, Titania, Puck and the fairies, and through spells and curses, the effects of the love-juice, the appearance of Bottom with an ass's head. The play is itself, of course, hypnotic, a kind of enchantment.

Some of these dualities have already been mentioned – light and dark, water and fire, true love and false love, Diana and Hecate, seeing and not seeing, visible and invisible, sleeping and waking. Others have been implied. It may now be useful to make some of these more explicit.

An obvious place to start is with the contrast between the sophistications and power structures of the city, where civilised behaviour is governed by codes of conduct (the "sharp Athenian law") accompanied by pomp and ceremony, and the world of Nature, the countryside or wood, with its own special wisdoms, where codes of conduct are put to the test (including the important one of chastity) and/or breaches of them are exposed. Pomp and ceremony can signify a proper decorum but sometimes can reveal themselves to be affectations. Athens thinks itself a place of reason and stability but these are threatened by the unreason of the young lovers; the wood on the other hand is a place where normality is suspended, a place of mischief, a dangerous environment to be in at night, a place where anything can happen: lovers quarrel, women are left unprotected, young men hint at rape, fight with swords, people are put under spells, an innocent workman is turned into an ass. Athens is the place of the court, of temples and nunneries; the wood a place of magic and fairies, where would-be actors rehearse in seclusion, but also where, in daylight, young people sometimes resort to empty their "bosoms of their counsel sweet" or go a-Maying in, as well as a place the privileged go a-hunting. Athens is where the nobility is attended on and amused by hard-handed men who fear for their lives if their performance displeases. Both are places of revels. The wood may also be seen as an equivalent to the Arcadias of pastoral writing, where the issue of Nature v. Nuture can be explored, an idealised landscape, a dream world indulged in by courtly imaginations. Arcadia is the classical equivalent of the Christians' Garden of Eden[1]. Helena's hymn to friendship in Act III is an Arcadian dream:

> We, Hermia, like two artificial gods
> Have with our needles created both one flower,
> Both on one sampler, sitting on one cushion,
> Both warbling of one song, both in one key,
> As if our hands, our sides, voices, and minds
> Had been incorporate. So we grew together
> Like to a double cherry, seeming parted
> But yet an union in partition,
> Two lovely berries moulded on one stem,
> So with two seeming bodies but one heart,
> Two of the first, like coats in heraldry
> Due but to one, but crownèd with one crest.
>   (Act III, scene 2, 203-14)

Shakespeare's wood is, as commentators insist, an English woodland remembered from a Warwickshire childhood – a different, though parallel, kind of idealisation. Nonetheless, there is a hint, in Titania's long speech in Act II, of the Garden of Eden in her accusing Oberon:

And this same progeny of evils
Comes from our debate, from our dissension.
We are their parents and original.

(Act II, scene 1, 115-17)

where an analogy with Adam and Eve and Original Sin is, I feel,
clearly implied. The whole of the speech is concerned with a kind of
paradise lost asking to be regained. Hermia, we may remember, wakes
violently from a nightmare containing a serpent (she also at one
point justly calls Demetrius a serpent) and the fairies cast a spell to
keep away "spotted snakes with double tongue" which Freud and
Jung would doubtless interpret as sexual. For present purposes let's
just register there are nasties as well as fairies at the bottom of the
garden!

For the lovers, the wood is sometimes a heaven, sometimes a
hell. Helena (who has been sufficiently undermined to think herself
ugly) follows Demetrius into it to make "a heaven of hell".
Paradoxically her love for him causes him to hate her, though she
grows fonder from being abused. Demetrius is less of a nice guy
than Lysander. He has already accused Demetrius of being a "spotted
and inconstant man" (spotted here means tainted and is also a pre-
echo of the "spotted snakes with double tongue") for having won the
"soul" (never a word to take lightly) of Helena even before the play
opens – a thing he confesses to Theseus at the end:

The object and the pleasure of mine eye,
Is only Helena. To her, my lord,
Was I betrothed ere I saw Hermia.

(Act IV, scene 1, 169-71)

Hermia, even before entering the wood, tells us

Before the time I did Lysander see
Seemed Athens as a paradise to me.
O then, what graces in my love do dwell
That he hath turned a heaven unto a hell?

(Act I, scene 1, 204-7)

It is a place to get lost in, of entanglements (being torn by briars)
and disentanglements (waking into truth), of temptations and

disappointments. Helena, the most ill-treated, can't wait to get back to the sanity of Athens:

> O weary night! O long and tedious night,
>   Abate thy hours, shine comforts from the East,
> That I may back to Athens by daylight
>   From these that my poor company detest.
>
> (Act III, scene 2, 431-4)

Ironically, the wood becomes (at least in his remembrance) a paradise for Bottom:

> Be kind and courteous to this gentleman.
> Hop in his walks and gambol in his eyes;
> Feed him with apricocks and dewberries,
> With purple grapes, green figs, and mulberries.
> The honey bags steal from the humble bees,
> And for night-tapers crop their waxen thighs
> And light them at the fiery glow-worms' eyes
> To have my love to bed and to arise;
> And pluck the wings from painted butterflies
> To fan the moonbeams from his sleeping eyes.
> Nod to him, elves, and do him courtesies.
>
> (Act III, scene 1, 159-69)

To be addressed as "gentleman" and attended on with "courtesies" is real promotion, a very heaven! He is being treated like a king. Stanley Wells says of Titania's infatuation for him:

> Bottom, fool that he is, and metamorphosed into an ass, can see that her love for him is unreasonable; but he is not such a fool as to reject it.

It is a standard feature of comedy to find generations in opposing camps. In *A Midsummer Night's Dream* we have a contrast between the older generation of Theseus and Hippolyta and the younger lovers, complicated by the opposition of daughter and father (Hermia and Egeus) as well as conflict between the suitors and one-time friends.

Theseus has wooed Hippolyta, Queen of the Amazons, with his

sword and won her love doing her injuries. Paradoxically, enemies are turned into partners. The play does not to my mind – though to feminist critics it does – suggest anything other than a nobility and the achievement of a peace in the relationship. It should perhaps be read as Shakespeare adding background information from memories of his reading without attaching a great deal of significance to it. Theseus simply overrides what, to modern ears, may sound offensive by saying

> But I will wed thee in another key:
> With pomp, with triumph, and with revelling.
>
> (Act I, scene 1, 18-19)

… the triumph being the happiness determined by and to be celebrated in the forthcoming wedding and not, I feel, a declaration of male authority – despite Theseus' endorsement of Egeus' rights of ownership over Hermia. It doesn't necessarily imply an enforced submission on the part of Hippolyta. The relationship between her and the Duke is, I think, meant to be looked upon as that between two noble equals with genuine experience of life (including earlier lovers) who now in their maturity have settled for a pacific life, for each other, and for a life aimed at stability tempered by reason – in other words, an exemplary relationship based on amity. As Harold Bloom amusingly puts it:

> In Plutarch's *Life of Theseus*, read by Shakespeare in Sir Thomas North's version, Theseus is credited with many 'ravishments', cheerfully itemized … by Oberon, who assigns Titania the role of bawd, guiding the Athenian hero to his conquests, herself doubtless included. Though Titania will retort 'These are the forgeries of jealousy', they are just as persuasive as her visions of Oberon 'versing love/To amorous Phillida', and enjoying 'the bouncing Amazon', Hippolyta. The Theseus of the *Dream* appears to have retired from womanizings into rational respectability, with its attendant moral obtuseness. Hippolyta, though championed as a victim by feminist critics, shows little aversion to being wooed by the sword and seems content to dwindle into Athenian domesticity after her exploits with Oberon, although she retains a vision of her own, as will be seen.

However, rather than over-psychologise what is little more than sketched in, it may simply be more useful to see Theseus and Hippolyta as figures in a pageant than as characters with full lives.

The opposition between Egeus and Hermia is what kick-starts the action. He has, as we pointed out earlier, right on his side. Modern readers and audiences are rightly appalled by the severity of the Athenian law. However, we have to take it as given that children are supposed to obey their fathers (consider what happens to Ophelia in *Hamlet* and Cordelia in *King Lear*) as guardians of their virginity (think of Prospero and Miranda in *The Tempest*). As we can see, conflict between freedom of choice and filial obedience is something Shakespeare continually takes on board. It is put succinctly by Desdemona after eloping with Othello:

> My noble father,
> I do perceive here a divided duty.
> To you I am bound for life and education;
> My life and education learn me
> How to respect you. You are the lord of duty,
> I am hitherto your daughter. But here's my husband,
> And so much duty as my mother showed
> To you, preferring you before her father,
> So much I challenge that I may profess
> Due to the Moor my lord.
>
> (Act I, scene 3, 178-87)

What we find difficult is the fact that insisting on the penalty of the law Egeus is made to sound cold-hearted, unloving, unfatherly. But what matters to Shakespeare is to show us the Duke in control, a leader, strict but also wise … even if to modern ears it all sounds unnecessarily severe. However, Theseus does give Hermia, and not Egeus, – albeit a sternly limited one – a choice. Worse things happen in fairy stories. Egeus has no real reasons for preferring Demetrius, unless they are pecuniary ones, and ignores the fact that Lysander and the Duke both know Demetrius has "Made love to Nedar's daughter, Helena". "Made love" does not, of course, carry our modern meaning of having sex with.

Egeus is still pursuing the law when the lovers are eventually discovered by Theseus and his attendants out hunting:

I beg the law, the law upon his head.
They would have stolen away, they would, Demetrius,
Thereby to have defeated you and me –
You of your wife, and me of my consent –
Of my consent that she should be your wife.

(Act IV, scene 1, 154-8)

This time he makes Lysander his target. In any case, Demetrius now confesses he was already betrothed to Helena "ere I saw Hermia". And the matter is summarily dismissed with Theseus' "Egeus, I will overbear your will". What was once life-threatening becomes life-enhancing. The wood turns out to have been a place of healing.

Obvious qualities found in opposition and already implied are: mortals and spirits, mortals and beasts, harmless things and dangerous things, reason and madness, love and jealousy, love and hate, life and death.

It is time to think of the differences in behaviour of males and females.

Notes

[1] See Milton's adaptation of pastoral in *Paradise Lost*.

10

A Scandal On My Sex

A Midsummer Night's Dream is also a play about power – who owns and who exercises it and to what purpose and with what effect. We know that Nature has power – benign and malign – and that it is controlled by capricious deities and the spirits who animate it. There is the power that comes from the knowledge of secret sources – herbs and flowers with transforming effects, the right words for spells and songs. We have only to remember the story of Marlowe's Faustus or think of Prospero in *The Tempest* to know how attracted to secret sources Elizabethans were. Magic is a form of power; it can bring about transformations. The aim of alchemy was to transform base metals into gold.

Man thinks he has power over Nature – in our play, hunting might be seen as symbolic of this. Sometimes, however, human beings are the playthings of Nature – like the lovers in the wood – witness Puck's getting things wrong. And there are, in the play, tensions between confidence in exercising power, the capriciousness of the immortals, and human frailty and vulnerability.

Oberon and Titania wield magical power and have attendants (who possess the enviable power of flight) to assist them. In the same way Elizabethans considered Theseus and Hippolyta historical figures, so they believed fairies to have a real existence as guardians of the secret sources mentioned above – though it must be continually pointed out that Shakespeare's fairies are somewhat removed from the world of folk lore so as to appear his own invention. Titania's train are by no means impish nor are they merely decorative: they have functions and, like good servants, they carry out tasks conscientiously. Their society too is hierarchically structured and highly ritualised. Oberon is a king and Titania a queen: the two of them give commands which they expect to be unquestioningly obeyed. They obviously parallel Theseus and Hippolyta and, in many productions, the roles are indeed played by the same actors – underscoring the notion that the audience has dreamt the play. In the dissension between them (and this tells us marriages are not necessarily happy-ever-after arrangements), we witness what appears to be, to all intents and purposes, a contest of equals. Like Lysistrata, Titania withholds her sexual favours in an attempt to persuade Oberon to give up his case against her. It is a weapon. He has Puck and love-in-idleness on his side. The dissension is also a measure of the power they have, in that it has global consequences.

What they are quarrelling about is not easy to explain. What it concerns is the ownership of the changeling boy. Oberon may be said to be simply wanting something he can't have; on the other hand he may also be justified. Titania too puts up a convincing case for keeping the child: the mother was not only a devoted member of her order but a companion, the birth to the child causing her death. Titania claims she is acting out of loyalty and duty:

> ... she, being mortal, of that boy did die,
> And for her sake do I rear up her boy;
> And for her sake I will not part with him.
>
> (Act II, scene 1, 134-6)

It is easy to portray her as the one wronged. Oberon has kept on pestering her: "with thy brawls thou hast disturbed our sport" (again, the motif of intrusion). It is these brawls according to her that have caused a revolt in Nature. However, she does also suggest this is the responsibility of both of them (again, the theme of amity or mutuality): they are the "parents and original" of a "progeny of evils". But the language she uses, particularly in her descriptions of the child's mother, emphasises conception and gestation, and may be said to give a strong impression of a wish she had conceived the child herself. Is it this Oberon is jealous of? Love that should be directed to him has been diverted to the changeling? Has Titania been ignoring him?

Changelings were the young of mortals stolen by the fairies and Oberon does state the child was "stolen" from an Indian king. Titania offers what seems to be quite another explanation. It is difficult to decide who is telling the truth. I have even met the suggestion that the votaress may have been raped by the Indian King. Kott goes as far as to make the point that the play would in no way be damaged if Shakespeare had omitted this whole business. But it is there in the play asking to be understood.

Oberon seems clearly outraged by his wife's stubbornness in allowing the child to come between them (another instance of intrusion). She has forsworn his bed ... this at a time when coupling in marriage is about to be celebrated and blessed. It was for this purpose the fairies have travelled to Athens. She considers the boy her "young squire"; Oberon calls him "her page" but thinks he should be part of his own retinue. She is adamant; "fairy land buys not this child of me". Do we accept Kott's view she is acting out of spite?

It is not difficult to see Oberon as asserting male authority. He can be made to sound imperious. (Titania too sounds imperious when she wants to be – remember she tells Bottom he has to stay with her whether he wants to or not). He accuses her of "pride" and calls her a "rash wanton". As accusations of promiscuity are made on both sides, one can't help feeling a bit like a policeman called in to investigate a 'domestic'. Perhaps we can go along with Harold Bloom, one of the few critics to tackle the problem of the changeling child, who considers Oberon maintaining "an innocent assertion of sovereignty" in a custody dispute. He goes on to suggest that even though the two immortals have no male heir, and no need of one, Oberon still has "paternal aspirations". He concludes:

> To exclude Oberon from the child's company is therefore not just a challenge to male authority, it is a wrong done to Oberon, and one that he must reverse and subsume in the name of the legitimacy in leadership with Titania. As Oberon says, it is an 'injury'.

If we take the word "injury" at face value the conclusion must be that Oberon feels his wife has on this occasion gone too far. His feelings are strong enough to provoke a kind of revenge. Unless you are one of those who feel that having her fall in love with an ass is a gross sexual insult (there are productions that turn Bottom into a vile caricature of animal lust), you might view it in the end as little more than a relatively harmless prank whose effects are, ultimately, beneficent. After all, Bottom's role in it is more passive than shockingly active. At the same time, remember, Oberon is actively busy on behalf of love – benevolently (despite Puck's error) helping confused lovers to recognise their true partners and achieve the mutuality (Elyot's "equity") that is their goal.

And clearly he softens. In Act III he says (lovingly?) "I'll to my Queen and beg her Indian boy" … not demand but beg. He later reports:

> I then did ask of her her changeling child,
> Which straight she gave me, and her fairy sent
> To bear him to my bower in Fairyland.
>
> (Act IV, scene 1, 58-60)

… not demand but ask. Is this an assertion of masculine will or the restoration of the proper order of things … is the one a requirement of the other? Has she simply surrendered or is this an occasion of restored mutual understanding, the achievement of amity? Is she, like Hippolyta, now happy to be in a relationship of equals? We can only ask the questions. One thing we may notice is a parallel in the conflict of ownership in the Egeus/Hermia scene in which Egeus states "As she is mine, I may dispose of her" and Hermia's being overcome by a power that makes her bold enough to oppose his will.

Power, based on rationality, is invested in leaders, fathers, and enshrined in the law. The law is, ideally, controlled by just people of reason – reason being the God-given angelic quality that provides the motivations required to govern us wisely, as well as regulate our personal lives. Because of it we live in societies that aspire to the good life. The idealisations of pastoral – a form of aristocratic daydream – provide useful images of this.

Theseus is the guardian of Athenian law. But laws are transgressed; people in power are thwarted or themselves may abuse the law; Egeus rightly calls upon it when it's broken; Theseus ("being overfull of self affairs/My mind did lose it") has let his responsibilities momentarily slip (again a consequence of being in love) and doesn't see a connection between his "desires" and his asking Hermia to question hers ("examine well your blood" meaning both control your sexual urges and consider your familial status). Shakespeare often depicts leaders neglecting or failing in their responsibilities and explores the dilemmas that must inevitably arise when this occurs. In Theseus' case, however, it not a serious dereliction.

In the business of love, men are seen to be the ones who pursue, who woo and win. Helena complains:

> We cannot fight for love, as men may do;
> We should be wooed, and were not made to woo.
>
> (Act II, scene 1, 241-2)

Theseus has 'won' Hippolyta, and when the play opens we are meant, let me re-emphasise, to see that this is part of a code of honour. Nothing suggests the arrangement is other than mutual. She doesn't give any indication of demurring. In fact, she is not only his equal, she has, as we shall see, a voice that is respectfully listened to. Theirs is a relationship often described as heroic.

The wood is a great leveller, an equalising place. It is there Hermia and Helena let their hair down and show themselves at least on a par with the men. (Many of the women characters in Shakespeare's plays are strong, resourceful, and independent-minded). They are armed with their 'virtue' – Helena has "the rich worth of her virginity"; Hermia, when it comes to sleeping arrangements, insists on the separation that becomes "a virtuous bachelor and a maid" – though in some modern productions Lysander is eager to try it on, which goes against the grain of the play. Virginity and chastity nearly always have a sacral role in Shakespeare.

Helena's description of friendship (Act III, scene 2, 199-214) implies the ideal of reciprocity, a quality the play examines and tests and because we are in a romantic comedy we can be confident that, after being turned inside out, it will eventually be re-established ... with a little magical assistance. The relationship between Hermia and Lysander seems to come as a shock to Helena and is felt as a betrayal: Hermia is quite prepared to relinquish this best-friendship for love's sake, blithely declaring she will "seek new friends" – no wonder Helena feels slighted. In the subsequent emotional confusion, we see the women giving as good as they get in the comic spectacle of a slanging match. Helena ends up stating that Hermia was "a vixen when she went to school". So much for the bonds of friendship! The men too are combative, challenging each other with swords, while at the same time showing themselves up in being nowhere near as honourable or as brave as they pretend. In fact, one could easily argue that Bottom on the subject of swords, lions, and ladies is more chivalrous than they. Demetrius, for example, taunts Helena with ungallant suggestions about the rich worth of her virginity and cruelly declares "I'll run from thee and hide me in the brakes,/And leave thee to the mercy of wild beasts". Weakness and vulnerability are certainly not the prerogative of the women. Both sexes can be equally silly and duplicitous. Comedy, as ever, exposing the disparity between what people pretend to be and what they really are. Theseus is not entirely above reproach in this respect either: the prospect of his marriage has made him temporarily neglectful. Being "overfull of self affairs,/My mind did lose it" he says of his previous knowledge of Demetrius' involvement with "Nedar's daughter, Helena". His mind then goes back to Hippolyta ("What cheer, my love?"), suddenly aware he has been neglecting *her*.

It is said by almost all commentators that the lovers are hardly differentiated – conventional figures from love stories, their characterisation left deliberately sketchy; almost to the point of seeming neutral: Hermia small, dark, sometimes peevish but generally likeable; Helena, tall, fair, easily put-upon; Demetrius testy; Lysander perhaps languid but with a whiff of humour. That they are hardly distinguishable is the point. Kott goes as far as to say the lovers are exchangeable. Shakespeare is not so much interested in their psychologies as in what they represent and embody – namely that "the truth, reason, and love keep little company together". The play is less motivated by character than by outside agencies – the fairies, the moon. As a consequence, as M.C. Bradbrook points out, a "symmetrical grouping of lovers ... allows the characters to be developed only in shallow relief."

Theseus and Hippolyta are the only ones, among the couples, not affected by moon-madness. They make entry into the wood only in daylight. They are warriors with a long history and their marriage can be seen as political, an act of state ... or, as with Othello, a desire to engage with the well-earned pleasures of retirement. As we have said, their maturity and stability provide the play with its frame. As well as representing justice (he sets the limit by which Hermia is to decide her fate), Theseus has power to command others: he has a

Master of Revels, Philostrate, to exact tribute for him from his subjects and respect for his status. Symbolising these, four entertainments are nominated, from which one only is 'preferred' (what does this say for the ones rejected?) A ritualised society, as Athens is shown to be, ensures the maintenance of power through ceremony – this is the only real view of the place we are given: a state of preparation (pomp, triumph, and revelling) for aristocratic marriages, enacted and celebrated – and parodied – in Act V.

The most potent source of power the play embodies is the transformative power of the imagination, the power of story. Shakespeare, tongue-in-cheek, describes his play in terms of "a weak and idle theme/No more yielding than a dream". But dreams have their own reality and strength.

The play of the "mechanicals" (this disparaging word is Puck's, who clearly has no great regard for mortals and their ways)[1] is a commitment to the power of the imagination. They put on a story. It is also, we must not forget, hedged round with danger: it may not be 'preferred'; it may cause the nobles offence ("they would have no more discretion but to hang us", warns Bottom); it might be mocked; and the performers could well forfeit the sixpence a day that would make them for life. However, one gets the distinct impression, when all is said and done, that they are performing for the unadulterated pleasure of simply doing so. Collectively, they are the equivalent of the court jester – like Feste in *Twelfth Night* or the Fool in *Lear*, for whom the consequences of not pleasing are always hazardous but who, at their best are both entertaining and self-delighting. Given all this, their undertaking is, to say the least, an act of courage, in itself requiring admiration and applause.

Notes

[1] To Shakespeare's audience they were the professional clowns of the company. The stage direction for Act III, scene 1, states "Enter the clowns: Bottom, Quince, Snout, Starveling, Flute, and Snug."

11

According To The Scrip

What characterises *The most lamentable comedy and most cruel death of Pyramus and Thisbe* is: (a) the obvious literalism with which it is rehearsed and performed; (b) how wonderfully eager the performers are; (c) how ill-equipped they are in mounting it and understanding what they are actually doing with it; (d) how innocent it all is. It is ironic that literalism and imagination, contrasted in the play, should produce a highly-imaginative experience. Like Doctor Johnson's definition of marriage, it represents a triumph of hope over experience.

If *A Midsummer Night's Dream* has elements of the courtly entertainments called masques, then this aspect may be said to constitute an anti-masque.

The story of Pyramus and Thisbe on which play the 'mechanicals' perform is based is, as already noted, taken from Ovid's *Metamorphoses* – though Quince (did he write the script?) is the only one who seems to know this or at least that it already exists as a story. It is a tale of lovers thwarted by parental prohibition and dying for love and can be thought of as a parody of *Romeo and Juliet*, which Shakespeare had not long written. It is also where the action of *A Midsummer Night's Dream* might have arrived but for the lovers' escape into the wood. In addition, it is a burlesque of various kinds of crude dramaturgy (M.C. Bradbrook links it to the bombast of an earlier play, *King Cambyses* of 1569, which Shakespeare mentions by title in *Henry IV, Part 2*). And, of course, it can't really be said to be an appropriate offering in the celebrations of a wedding feast. It is in every way the opposite of the play the audience of *A Midsummer Night's Dream* is attending. It is badly written and badly performed. It is also a triumph.

It seems to me quite wrong to me to portray Bottom as arrogant and overbearing – even worse to coarsen him into a symbol of lust. He, more than Quince, is the driving force behind the rehearsing and performing of the interlude. Equipped with a totally ingenuous estimation of self-worth, he has at the same time an overwhelming desire to give more than his best. For unimpeachable reasons, he simply wants to do everything himself and do it splendidly. It is not that he mistrusts his companions but more a case of unrestrained and incorrigible dynamism. He is fearless where they tend to be timorous – his only fear that of causing offence.

The play does not mock him: he is admired by his fellows, even when he covets their parts or tries to take over their jobs – though there are productions in which Quince is sometimes given a tetchy impatience. When they think he's gone missing, we hear them speak nothing but praise: Quince says "You have not a man in all Athens able to discharge Pyramus but he", to which Flute adds "No, he hath simply the best wit of any handicraft man in Athens". We may smile at such pronouncements.

Bottom is no Malvolio ... though there are those who would see him as a satirical portrait of a Puritan. The epithet "Bully" has nothing to do with bullying; rather it denotes admiration. He is, as it were, a first among equals. Quince thinks well enough of him to allot him the grandest part, that of Pyramus. As Bloom tells us:

> Bottom is heroically sound in his goodness of heart, his
> bravery, his ability to remain himself in any circumstance, his
> refusal to panic or even be startled ...

He is only silly in the sense of the word discussed earlier. Most audiences – unless a director wants to emphasise "mortal grossness" – applaud him as the play's lovable centre. He is a vehicle *for* satire rather than an object of it.

The "hempen homespuns" (again the disparaging description is Puck's) are men "thought fit in all Athens" to play in the interlude. It is hard to know whose estimation this represents but the joke is, if these are the best what can be said for the rest. This prompts the thought that in a sense the wood represents ignorance. If Oberon and Titania go there, among other things, to put their quarrel right, and the lovers undertake a rite of passage from love-madness to a potential love-sanity, then it is also true of the simple workmen that they go into the wood to confront their own species of ignorance. The names Shakespeare gives them are sympathetic, not only suggesting a certain homeliness but, in Starveling, perhaps poverty too – though it may simply mean he is thin and maybe starves himself. Like the lovers, their characters are merely sketched in: Flute just reaching puberty, Snug "slow of study", Snout unimaginative, Starveling a bit of a pessimist. They are ambitiously taking on, for the best of all reasons, something beyond them in which they are inevitably bound to fail. But what a triumphant failure it turns out to be! It should be measured not in terms of success but enthusiastic aspiration. With no hint of affectation, their play confers roles on them above their station and for the most part they make manly efforts to carry it off. It is much to their credit that they do this despite the fact they "have never laboured in their minds till now".

When we first meet them, it is Bottom's enthusiasm that carries all before, ensuring we are not overcritical of their ignorance (unlike perhaps the supercilious nobles later) but remain sympathetic. The 'mechanicals' are amateurs in the true sense.

And their first meeting provides some of the play's important keynotes: a sense of the paradoxical ("his wedding day at night"; the "lamentable comedy", roaring "as gently as any sucking dove"); a connection between love and death ("A lover that kills himself, most gallant, for love"); deceptions necessary to the creation of illusion ("You shall play it in a mask, and you may speak as small as you will", "What beard were best to play it in?"); parody (the ear-splitting alliteration and jingly rhyming in "Ercles' vein"); mistakes arising from ignorance ("What is Thisbe? – a wandering knight?"); and things said innocent of their meaning (French crowns having no hair at all being an allusion to the pox).

It is in the wood that literalism rears its head. Bottom has had time to study the script and spot dangers in it. This, in my view, is no mere forelock-tugging deference but rather a genuine sensitivity, one that, ironically, comes from an imagination that is creative ... ironically because, at first sight, it makes the would-be actors seem fearful of being able to control the great power of the imagination they let loose. In fact you might say it adds another dimension to their play ... an intersecting of various realities (the very stuff of *A Midsummer Night's Dream*) as they step in and out of it. The sword that kills Pyramus is, before we start, rendered harmless, the lion made toothless, an absurd parody of the moon has to be introduced, and a wall supplied whose fingers form a chink. We find ourselves wondering when and where do art and reality come together (in their play the word "truth" is heard several times) and when do they run counter to one another and cancel each other out.

Once the details of performance are satisfactorily settled, they sit (though actually Quince had said "we will do it in action as we will do it before the Duke") to rehearse. As soon as they get going, the invisible Puck intrudes himself and quickly (swiftness being a fairy characteristic) conceives the trick he will play on Bottom, taking his cue from the weaver's exit-line "And by and by I will to thee appear", putting a gleam in his eye.

12

Bottom, Thou Art Translated

And so everyone according to his cue.

Shakespeare is fond of drawing attention to the fact – it's a species of punning – we are in a theatre watching a play. The audience, enjoying the impishness, become allies of Puck ("I'll be an auditor – /An actor too, perhaps, if I see cause") – who enters on cue, invisible to the would-be actors. He would, I'm sure, be looking at and treating the audience as his accomplices. The fact that we see him and those acting the part of the homespuns must pretend they don't draws us in. Shakespeare's mastery of stagecraft is confirmed in this by being wonderfully self-parodied.

Puck, tipping us the wink, makes a perfect exit with the words "A stranger Pyramus than e'er played here". Note that it is Puck's decision Bottom becomes an ass, not Oberon's. Pyramus has exited for no given reason but done so with a promise to return "by and by" (explained after the event by Quince as his going to "see a noise"). Thisbe does *not* come in on cue ("Must I speak now?") but Pyramus does, *exactly* so, bearing the ass's head his fellows and the audience can see but he cannot. This is also, of course, a parody of Acteon who, when turned into a stag, retained his human consciousness. Shakespeare has, with beautiful precision, stage-managed a comic catastrophe. With a sequence of superb timings, the homespuns' rehearsal is thrown into confusion. Bottom's fellow actors rush out in disorder and fear ... though it should be noted that two of them return briefly – Snout disbelievingly and Quince momentarily overcoming his fear to give his old friend a benediction: "Bless thee, Bottom! Bless thee! Thou art translated!"

Bottom, with no reason to think so, imagines it's a plot to frighten him (his fellow actors, as we have noticed, are much more timorous than he): he bravely sticks around in hope of demonstrating to them that *he's* not afraid. He walks up and down, singing a slightly bawdy song (though whether he is aware of its bawdiness is open to debate) that treats of more homely birds than the lullaby concerning Philomel, the nightingale (though her story, remember, involves a rape), that not long before had induced sleep in Titania. It is this bawdy song that *wakes* her and causes her to say:

> I pray thee, gentle mortal, sing again!
> Mine ear is much enamoured of thy note.
> So is mine eye enthrallèd to thy shape,
> And thy fair virtue's force perforce doth move me
> On the first view to say, to swear, I love thee.
> (Act III, scene 1, 130-34)

Bradbrook informs us that "shape" is a technical term for an actor's costume – which we might care to remember when we come to discuss Theseus' speech in Act V in which he dilates on the function of the imagination. But the words to notice here are "gentle" and "virtue". Both raise Bottom to the status of gentleman.

Ironically Bottom, so to speak, keeps his head; he replies in prose, in the language of homely wisdom, with the wit of a clown:

> Methinks, mistress, you should have little reason for that.
> And yet, to say the truth, reason and love keep little company
> together nowadays – the more the pity that some honest
> neighbours will not make them friends. – Nay, I can gleek
> upon occasion.
> (Act III, scene 1, 135-39)

(gleek meaning to joke, and notice he allies himself with neighbours who are honest). He addresses Titania as "mistress" as if she were any woman he might meet along the road. He ignores (some might say he is insensitive to) her advances, claiming he has enough wit to know how to get out of the wood. This, and what follows, gives the lie to those who would treat him as a symbol of bestial lust. The strain of parody continues. It is when she summons Peaseblossom, Cobweb, Moth, and Mustardseed and tells them to be courteous to him – in other words she provides him with a court – that Bottom is in his element. As Middleton Murry points out "Bully Bottom behaves like a fairy gentleman when he is in proper company". This "proper company" is not really Titania but the fairies attending him at her behest. I am tempted to describe him as a big soft kid – by which I mean he is soft-hearted, one of the world's great innocents. Even with his court around him, Bottom betrays the deference he is used to giving his betters: he calls his attendants "your worships"; Peaseblossom is "honest gentleman". But what we are aware of is that he feels at ease in this company. In Bloom's words: "What we ... have is a gentle, good-natured Bottom, who is rather more inclined to the company of elves ... than to the madly infatuated Titania."

When we meet them again in Act IV, the ingenuous Bottom continues to show more interest in his attendant fairies than in Titania:

> Titania: Come, sit thee down upon this flowery bed
> While I thy amiable locks do coy,
> And stick muskroses in thy sleek, smooth head.
> And kiss thy fair large ears, my gentle joy.
>
> Bottom: Where's Peaseblossom?
>
> (Act IV, scene 1, 1-6)

Titania's words are a parody of Petrarchan love poetry: It is important to stress that the activity with flowers suggests idealised romance rather than something overtly sexual. It should be remembered that lovers in the Pertrachan mode are usually more in love with love, more interested in being ennobled through their adoration of the beloved than in consummation. In any case, the words are lost on Bottom. When asked whether he'd like to hear music he claims he has "a reasonable good ear for music" and asks for the homely tongs and bones. This is not the ass-head talking but Bully Bottom, the 'mechanical': music to him is a social activity. He has merely been translated physically. The play uses music to magical effect: it sends to sleep and it awakens. And at this moment of expectation of plenty Bottom simply falls asleep. So much for gross sexual appetite.

Fairy time and mortal time, we have said, are different. When Bottom wakes, it is into what he thinks is the instantaneous continuation of the rehearsal: "When my cue comes, call me, and I will answer". The interim has been a dream.

13

The Concord Of This Discord

The wood, we know, is a place of ritual observances. It is associated
with Midsummer, with Maying, and St Valentine ... with, on the
positive side, love, friendship, healing; on the negative, madness,
dissension, witchcraft. When day returns (Puck advises his master
"Fairy king, attend, and mark:/I do hear the morning lark") things
are put right again. Oberon and Titania are now "new in amity" and
Bottom's ass's head is removed. All of this is celebrated with a ritual
dance – itself an enactment of patterned order – which rocks the
ground and therefore, like a mini-earthquake presumably wakes the
lovers. The fairies, in fairy time, needing to follow the moon (Puck
tells us that fairies "run ... From the presence of the sun/Following
darkness like a dream"), fly off to circle the globe (we know Puck
can do this in 40 minutes) in order that they may be back for the
midnight of the next night's festivities:

> Now thou and I are new in amity,
> And will tomorrow midnight solemnly
> Dance in Duke Theseus' house triumphantly,
> And bless it to all fair prosperity.
> There shall the pairs of faithful lovers be
> Wedded with Theseus all in jollity.
>
> (Act IV, scene 1, 86-91)

... midnight being the time kindly protective spirits are always
needed, the time of crucial changes. The rhyming in the above
passage, like the beat of the dance, may be seen and felt as an
enactment of concord.

They are immediately replaced by daytime's protectors, Theseus and Hippolyta. The music accompanying Oberon and Titania's pre-dawn dance ("whiche betokeneth concorde")[1] is replaced by the sound of horns and hounds: it is as if the return of the sun, in the "vaward of the day", is being ceremoniously welcomed. With the words "now our observation is performed" Theseus makes it clear that a ritual event – almost certainly to do with the Summer Solstice (though Wells connects it with the "observance to a morn of May" mentioned in Act I) – has taken place, presumably at dawn. The couple are not just out to take the air or enjoy themselves hunting: they are observing custom, propitiating the gods.

It is only after this 'observation' Theseus shows off his hounds to his wife-to-be and, in keeping with the way *A Midsummer Night's Dream* continually plays with paradox (what Wells calls the "yoking of opposites" and "agreement that can include disagreement"), asks us to listen to the "musical confusion/Of hounds and echo in conjunction". Hippolyta certainly finds the sound congenial: it brings back memories of hunting in Sparta with Hercules and Cadmus:

> I never heard
> So musical a discord, such sweet thunder.
>
> (Act IV, scene 1, 116-7)

A point of mutuality is gained when he tells her "My hounds are bred out of the Spartan kind". What we have here then is a sharing of experiences, the kind of amity recently achieved and now shared by the fairy King and Queen.

There is something symphonic in this harmonising of hounds, horns and their echoes. It celebrates earthly power, makes thunder sweet; it also emulates the perfect concord of the divine music only God and the angels ever hear, in the same way that Oberon and Titania's dance does. When Theseus espies the awakened lovers, he asks "How comes this gentle concord in the world?"

Notes

[1] Sir Thomas Elyot, *Boke named the Governour* (1531) quoted by T.S. Eliot in *Burnt Norton*:

> In that open field
> If you do not come too close, if you do not come too close,

On a summer midnight, you can hear the music
Of the weak pipe and the little drum
And see them dancing around the bonfire
The association of man and woman
In daunsinge, signifying matrimonien –
A dignified and commodious sacrament.
Two and two, necessary conjunction,
Holding eche other by the hand or arm
Whiche betokeneth concorde.

14

But A Dream

When he wakes, Bottom is in much the same condition as the lovers – total disbelief. The line between appearance and reality has become fluid: "Are you sure/That we are awake?" asks Demetrius, who thinks he's suddenly become short-sighted; Hermia imagines she's seeing double; Bottom knows he's been gifted with "a most rare vision". He and the lovers have been changed into something rich and strange. The 1998 Hollywood film directed by Michael Hoffman has Theseus and Hippolyta discover the lovers in a state of undress behind a hedge, clearly indicating they are sexually compromised. This goes against the grain of the play where virginity is revered, regarded as sacred, and sex is meant only for marriage. If Bottom has been changed it is in this: he has been blessed (we remember Quince's benediction) – and he knows it. It is something which will stay life-enhancingly with him for the rest of his days, something that deserves to be made into a ballad (it has actually been enacted in the very play we have been witnessing) so that others can share the wonderment. In describing it, Bottom gets his senses in a deliciously delirious confusion … it is as if his mind is racing and he can't get his words right. In a sense, he will go on living the dream. Like us, he'll carry the dream away with him. Harold Bloom considers Bottom:

> Shakespeare's Everyman, a true original, a clown rather than a fool or jester. He is a wise clown, though he smilingly denies his palpable wisdom, as if his innocent vanity did not extend to such pretension.

And so he is.

The lovers, having hopefully achieved amity or at least now

knowing what to aim for, are married ... their couplings blessed by religion ("For in the temple by and by with us/These couples shall eternally be knit") but just as importantly by the fairies. As Hermia says, "everything seems double" ... because that's precisely what it is. A case of double indemnity, we might say. You may recall what I said earlier about what we miss if we do not consider the context of eternity.

Theseus and Hippolyta can settle back to governing Athens, after a fortnight (and here's another seeming paradox) of solemnity consisting of "nightly revels and new jollity". The dream, it would seem, is to go on without us.

But not before the nobles have been entertained by a most lamentable comedy and a Bergomask dance.

15

Hot Ice And Wondrous Strange Snow

The play offered by the "hard-handed men that work in Athens" (the description is the unctuous Philostrate's) is mocked as "a nothing" by him. But, as with Egeus, he is overruled. In both cases the aim is to show Theseus as the good ruler – wiser, more compassionate than his advisors:

> I will hear that play,
> For never anything can be amiss
> When simpleness and duty tender it.
>
> (Act V, scene 1, 81-3)

Hippolyta is compassionate too but in a different kind:

> I love not to see wretchedness o'ercharged,
> And duty in his service perishing.
>
> (Act V, scene 1, 85-86)

The reassurances her husband gives her ("Love, therefore, and tongue-tied simplicity/In least speak most to my capacity") may well partly allude to Elizabeth I who was said to behave in a similarly generous way toward her subjects. And it is just as well he does. The audience has been set up for the performance of this interlude, fully expecting it to be a gloriously well-meaning shambles. The nobles don't know what they are in for. They are simply entertained but the audience, already primed, is treated doubly to something hilarious and wonderfully human. What to them is little more than amusing, to the audience is a creative triumph. Not only is the lamentable comedy a marvellous burlesque of crudely written plays, with their melodramatic ranting and bewailings, their superfluous explaining of events, their bewailing imperatives ("O grim-looked night, O night so black of hue"), preponderance of adjectives and heavy-handed alliteration ("thy gracious, golden, glittering beams"), their bathos ("O dainty duck, O dear!"), their over-insistent rhyming ("Now am I dead,/Now am I fled"), blatant contradictions ("I see a voice. Now will I to the chink/To spy an I can hear my Thisbe's face") – it is also completely consonant with the devices and themes we have been exploring. It is a sort of waking dream, which we are being constantly and joyously manoeuvred in and out of. The great Shakespearean theme of appearance and reality is treated with such fluidity that we are continuously dazzled – like Hermia on waking, we see "things with parted eye/When everything seems double". Only it is more than this. It is seeing with kaleidoscopic vision. Bradbrook says:

> Plays which depicted the court – such as *Love's Labours Lost* – must have had something of a mirror function; and as we learn from the play within a play, a courtly audience was quite as likely to intervene as a popular one ... It is a part of the 'mirror' technique of the play within a play, where Bottom so laboriously makes everyone comfortable with explanations of the difference between life and art, and where the fun puts both players and audience together inside the jest of professional actors pretending to be mechanicals trying to be amateur actors before an unreal audience.

It goes without saying that a play about lovers disobeying their parents and dying for love (like Romeo and Juliet) offered by perhaps more accomplished actors would hardly have been thought suitable for a wedding-night feast. This clearly indicates that it is the human performance we are meant to value. It is the inept acting that keeps the tragic nature of the story at bay; willing suspension of disbelief is made impossible; the play does indeed provide tragical mirth. It also reminds us that *A Midsummer Night's Dream* could have had quite a different ending. It contains its own opposite.

Shakespeare is rarely satirical. If anything is satirised here it is the old-style drama not the performers, who keep comically stepping out of their roles to assure everybody who they really are. The courtly spectators are critical ... but it is not without some irony that their comments too give gratuitous explanations. Theseus, for example, tells us that Quince "doth not stand upon points" – in other words doesn't know where to put his full stops (as in the nursery riddle "I saw a peacock with a fiery tail/I saw a comet ...") But the nobles are not allowed to have it all their own way: their interventions, (what passes for aristocratic wit) are daringly corrected:

> Theseus: The wall, methinks, being sensible, should curse again.
>
> Bottom: No, in truth sir, he should not. 'Deceiving me' is Thisbe's cue. She is to enter now, and I am to spy her through the wall. You shall see – it will fall pat as I told you. Yonder she comes.
>
> (Act V, scene 1, 179-84)

Shakespeare may be satirising courtly wit but, if he is, it is gently done. Aristocrats were expected to amuse each other in this way. In the context determined by Theseus' amiability, it may be viewed as harmless ... it could perhaps even be argued that their willingness to enter the performance in the way they do is a kind of compliment. I have seen productions in which the nobles are more engrossed by the play than they seem to want to admit. On the other hand, it is possible to portray them as arrogantly supercilious ... though I don't feel this necessarily sorts with the play's overall tone.

16

That Yet We Sleep, We Dream

Was it a vision or a waking dream? *A Midsummer Night's Dream* inevitably teases us into metaphysical speculation. I am minded of an old *Goon Show* moment in which the famous Minnie Banister tells the redoubtable Henry Crun "Last night I had a lovely dream, Henry: I dreamt I was asleep". Or the ancient Chinese riddle that says "Last night I dreamt I was a butterfly. This morning I do not know if I am a man who dreamt he was a butterfly or a butterfly now dreaming he is a man."

Sleep and waking – but which comes first, which is our reality? Which do we trust as more real: reason or imagination, evidence of the senses or what can be proved? (Blake once stingingly wrote "What is now proved was once only imagin'd"). What happens when these things collide and fall to confusion? How do we find the concord of this discord? There is real sleep and induced sleep; real wakefulness and magically altered wakefulness. There is, as we have seen, a play within a play that is half performance and, because the illusion is constantly being interrupted, half something else. There is a woodland world of fairies, of airy spirits, music and of poetry made to intersect with mortal grossness and the 'real' world of pragmatic Athens ruled by a Duke who has difficulties acknowledging these. There is a vision of global disaster and the generous vision of a group of Athenian workmen attempting to cobble together a play in which the worlds of court and of Athens' back streets intersect. And it is imagination that makes it all possible.

A Midsummer Night's Dream is an engineered illusion. In the end its author, speaking through Puck, tells us we have dreamt the whole thing. We are awakened by our own applause and leave the theatre revivified. In other words the audience has undergone a metamorphosis.

Bottom wakes to joyous bewilderment and, like the Ancient Mariner, carries his dream with him; the lovers too:

> Demetrius: Do not you think
> The Duke was here, and bid us follow him?
>
> Hermia: Yea, and my father.
>
> Helena: And Hippolyta.
>
> Lysander: And he did bid us follow to the temple.
>
> Demetrius: Why, then, we are awake. Let's follow him,
> And by the way let's recount our dreams.
>   (Act IV, scene 1, 193-98)

Their dreams only become 'real' when they are verbalised – in other words metamorphosed. It is the very process of poetry, as Theseus, despite himself, admits in his famous speech:

> I never may believe
> These antique fables, nor these fairy toys.
> Lovers and madmen have such seething brains,
> Such shaping fantasies, that apprehend
> More than cool reason ever comprehends.
> The lunatic, the lover, and the poet
> Are of imagination all compact.
> One sees more devils than vast hell can hold.
> That is the madman. The lover, all as frantic,
> Sees Helen's beauty in a brow of Egypt.
> The poet's eye, in a fine frenzy rolling,
> Doth glance from heaven to earth, from earth to heaven.
> And as imagination bodies forth
> The form of things unknown, the poet's pen
> Turns them to shapes, and gives to airy nothing
> A local habitation and a name.
> Such tricks hath strong imagination
> That if it would but apprehend some joy,

It comprehends some bringer of that joy,
Or in the night, imagining some fear,
How easy is a bush supposed a bear?

(Act V, scene 1, 2-22)

At first hearing, this sounds like Puritan distrust of the imagination, the notion that poetry is fiction ('feigning') and therefore sinful lies; it is also a direct criticism of the very play we are experiencing – and the one (the lamentable comedy) we are about to. In other words, he has no knowledge of the very things we have for two hours been seeing with our own eyes. Ovid is dismissed as "antique fables" and the fairy world has no existence. What he says of lovers and madmen is, of course, true (he has in his court four young lovers who have passed through their special kind of madness) but he purports to come at it from the viewpoint of "cool reason". He says of the lovers that their stories are more strange than true ... which simply means he has no way of assimilating such truth. His word "strange" brings to mind, as a corrective, Ariel's song in *The Tempest*:

Full fathom five thy father lies;
   Of his bones are coral made;
Those are pearls that were his eyes;
   Nothing of him that doth fade
But doth suffer a sea change
Into something rich and strange.

One of the problems with Theseus' speech is that it's often detached from its context, in which form it is made to support theories of poetic composition. In context it is highly sceptical, if not dismissive, and, as we have said, flies in the face of audience experience. We have been involved in "these fairy toys" and found that they are not toys (things of no significance) and if poets' eyes have to roll in a fine frenzy to produce such a play as we have been witnessing then give us more. Here is a case of Shakespeare putting some of his best poetry into the mouth of the 'wrong' person (as he teasingly does with Caliban in *The Tempest*). For what seems to happen is that either Shakespeare can't help intruding himself into the speech – particularly in the words "and gives to airy nothing/A local habitation and a name" (the job of prelapsarian Adam) – or he is undermining Theseus' rationality by ironically having him acknowledge the very transformative power of the "strong imagination" he is intent on denying. Bloom sees it this way:

> Theseus himself could be called, not unkindly, highly unimaginative, but there are two voices here, and one perhaps is Shakespeare's own, half-distancing itself from its own art, though declining also to yield completely to the patronizing Theseus. When he writes these lines, the lover sees Helen's beauty in a gypsy girl's brow, and yet the prophetic consciousness somewhere in Shakespeare anticipates Antony seeing Helen's beauty in Cleopatra.

("brow of Egypt" may well be a reference to colour of the skin, Cleopatra's "tawny front"). He goes on to say that to Shakespeare's contemporaries imagination was "'fantasy', a powerful but suspect faculty of the mind" and quotes Bacon to support this view:

> Neither is the Imagination simply and only a messenger; but is invested with or at leastwise usurpeth no small authority in itself, besides the duty of the message

Bloom's gloss on this is: "the mind for Bacon is the legitimate authority, and imagination should be content to be the mind's messenger, and to assert no authority for itself."

Theseus' speech is made in answer to Hippolyta's " 'Tis strange, my Theseus, that these lovers speak of." And, having listened to it patiently, she replies:

> But all the story of the night told over,
> And all their minds transfigured so together,
> More witnesseth than fancy's images,
> And grows to something of great constancy;
> But howsoever, strange and admirable.
>
> (Act V, scene 1, 23-7)

She will not give up her word "strange" nor the idea of transfiguration and growth. She clearly implies there are other ways of thinking and perceiving the world besides Theseus' rationality. As Bloom says: "Hippolyta's majestic gravity is an implicit rebuke to Theseus' scoffing at the poet's 'fine frenzy'".

If I were directing the play, the presentation of Theseus at this point might provide me with a problem. If, as we have said, his is a portrait of a kindly leader, a symbol of stability, his attitudes now would suggest a mind-set somewhat limited. In addition, his interjections during the performance of the lamentable comedy seem to contradict what he has had to say. He finds a place for imagination in that it can 'amend', make palatable. Now how much is condescension? Do we present Theseus and his aristocratic circle as supercilious and patronising, showing themselves up by the rudeness of their intrusive comments:

Lysander: This lion is a very fox for his valour.

Theseus: True; and a goose for his discretion.
(Act V, scene 1, 225-6)

The preferred play is there simply to stave off boredom – "this long age of three hours". Either that or provide an amusing interlude. It has not been chosen for its merit ... the other entertainments listed by Philostrate sound equally awful (one I'm sure is an in-joke: Orpheus, the archetypal poet, torn to pieces by "tipsy Bacchanals ... in their rage"). He does not recommend it. But the play of Pyramus and Thisbe, with its advertised contradictions, sounds just about entertaining enough to "ease the anguish of a torturing hour". When midnight arrives we are left with the judgement that "This palpable-gross play hath well beguiled/The heavy gait of night." (To be fair to Theseus, he does at the outset honour the "simpleness and duty" of the offering, and "well beguiled" can be taken as confirmation of this: that, even though the play itself is a travesty, he is appreciative of the homage and good efforts of his performing subjects).

But how do we square this with the behaviour of the courtly audience? Are we to indulge their wit as to the manner born?

It seems strangely inappropriate at this juncture, when everything is pleasure-driven, to introduce a sour note making the court hateful. And yet it is hard to feel comfortable with this sort of interchange:

Starveling as Moonshine: This lanthorn doth the hornèd
                           moon present.

Demetrius:	He should have worn the horns on his head.
Theseus:	He is no crescent, and his horns are invisible within the circumference.

(Act V, scene 1, 233-36)

... that demeaning suggestion that Starveling is a cuckold. Or this, picking up on Pyramus' word "die":

Demetrius:	No die, but an ace for him; for he is but one.
Lysander:	Less than an ace, man; for he is dead. He is nothing.
Theseus:	With the help of a surgeon he might yet recover, and prove an ass.

(Act V, scene 1, 299-301)

Harmless banter or distasteful hauteur? Is Hippolyta's "I am aweary of this moon. Would he would change" a sign of boredom or amorous titilation meant for her husband? Is he constrained by good manners merely in his answer "But yet in courtesy, in all reason, we must stay the time"?

It is possible to effect a compromise – to have the courtly audience imaginatively drawn into the performance they are watching, in keeping with the theme of mutuality we have discovered to be important to the play, and interpret their comments and those of the performers stepping out to answer them as a kind of reciprocity. (One should also note a kind of ironic reversal in that the play is in verse and we have the court speaking in prose).

Pyramus and Thisbe miraculously return to life and, just as in performances at the Globe, the play within a play ends with a dance, after which the iron tongue of midnight tolls out and the fairy protecting spirits reappear.

17

Hand In Hand With Fairy Grace

For the humans midnight brings an end to acting and dancing; it is now the witching hour; the fairies have tasks to perform, while the mortals go off to consummate their marriages and then to sleep … perchance to dream … with the promise of protection and the prospect of a fortnight more of revels. Pyramus and Thisbe have their memorial (like the statues promised the star-crossed lovers at the end of *Romeo and Juliet*): we are told "the wall is down that parted their fathers" … though they live on as Bottom and Flute – and in our memories – with sixpence a day in their pockets.

Not only did Keats intimately know this play, Blake did too. Parts of Puck's speech beginning "Now the hungry lion roars" are pure Blake. Night is the time predators appear and protectors of innocence are needed; the time for getting lost in mists and entangled in briars:

> When wolves and tigers howl for prey,
> They (angels) pitying stand and weep;
> Seeking to drive their thirst away,
> And keep them from the sheep.
> But if they rush dreadful,
> The angels, most heedful,
> Receive each mild spirit,
> New worlds to inherit.
>
> 'Night' from *Songs of Innocence*

The fairies are not things of daylight: they run from the sun and, as immortals, live in perpetual night … something I once had a taste of when flying back to England from Australia. Oberon gives us a beautiful image in the "glimmering light" of the "dead and drowsy fire" of vacated rooms. It's the fairies' time to be "frolic" (the seven-syllable lines they speak here come trippingly off the tongue) – to sing and dance (instances of concord and unity) and to bless. Oberon and Titania, it will be noticed, follow the proper procedure (in accordance with the doctrine of degree of a hierarchically-structured society) of themselves blessing the "best bride bed" – that of Theseus and Hippolyta. Puck (in his guise of Robin Goodfellow usually depicted holding a broom) fulfils his role of sweeping up the dust and refers to Theseus' palace as "this hallowed house", telling us it has been sanctified, made holy, a place where couples have been solemnly and eternally knit. The word "eternally" should not be missed. Shakespeare is subtly braiding together Christian and pagan. The fairies now play the role of guardian angels and will remain "until the break of day". Oberon and Titania propose a song (which the play, as we have it, does not provide) and a dance. The "field dew" is described as "consecrate" – another heavily-loaded religious word. The fatal sprinklings of Diana that turned Acteon into a stag have now become holy water and the baptismal water of the font that ensures any offspring the couples may have are also knit to eternity. The purpose of marriage to produce children is confirmed. True love is celebrated in terms of everlastingness – Oberon, in a quasi-priestly guise, using the words "ever" and "never". The children "Ever shall be fortunate", the couples three "Ever true in loving", Theseus "Ever shall in safety rest". And:

> Never mole, harelip, nor scar,
> Nor mark prodigious, such as are
> Despisèd in nativity,
> Shall upon these children be.

> (Act V, scene 1, 401-4)

The rhythmical pulse of the verse in this final scene is ritualistic: a benediction is being acted out. Another view of this might be that the rhythms are in keeping with fairy swiftness, brisk movement.

Puck's is the final voice – in racy octosyllabic couplets. Stepping forward, as Bottom had done, he directly addresses the audience, easing us out of the spell we have been under. We undergo a metamorphosis from illusion into everyday reality. His first line cuts through this illusion with the word "shadows". This not only means airy nothings, insubstantial beings, figments of our and the author's imaginations, but also real-life actors. This is also the meaning of "visions" in his fourth line. A richness of punning is going on: we have all been dreaming *A Midsummer Night's Dream*. And also a certain playful modesty – Puck ventriloquising Shakespeare. If the play hasn't entertained us, it can be dismissed as mere slumbering; it is, after all, but a "weak and idle theme". And if we didn't like it, well, be assured it will be better next time. In a sense, Puck is asking for a benediction on the play. The language is penitential: "offended"/ "mended"; "If you pardon, we will mend"; "We will make amends"; "Robin shall restore amends". Even the serpent from the Garden of Eden makes an appearance in the form of possible hissing:

> If we have unearnèd luck
> Now to scape the serpent's tongue
> We will make amends ere long.
>
> (Act V, scene 1, 422-24)

This direct address to the members of the audience acknowledges their importance as part of a creative partnership between them and the theatre. In Beryl Bainbridge's novel, *An Awfully Big Adventure*, about the Liverpool Playhouse, set in 1950, the stage director, Meredith, addresses the audience at the end of a performance reminding them that they:

> the audience, were what mattered, for it should never be forgotten that it was their patronage and applause which really kept the theatre alive.

In a less hackneyed way, Shakespeare too wishes to embrace his audience, to gratefully acknowledge their importance to him, to importune their approval and encouragement to go on writing and know they will come back for more.

The end of *A Midsummer Night's Dream* is similar to Prospero's *Epilogue* in *The Tempest* in its plea for forgiveness and prayer – to be signified in each case by applause – as a way of bringing the play to a close. Prospero tells his audience:

> And my ending is despair
> Unless I be relieved by prayer,

> Which pierces so that it assaults
> Mercy itself and frees all faults.
> As you from crimes would pardoned be,
> Let your indulgence set me free.

Shakespeare, in the case of *The Tempest,* is, most people like to imagine, saying farewell to his career as a dramatist; in *A Midsummer Night's Dream* he is a third of the way promising to do better.

The honesty ("as I am an honest Puck") is all – even if it has a twinkle in its eye.

Bibliography

Jonathan Bate, *The Genius of Shakespeare* (Picador, 1997)

Harold Bloom, *Shakespeare: the Invention of the Human* (Fourth Estate, 1998)

M.C. Bradbrook, *Shakespeare and Elizabethan Poetry* (Penguin, 1964)

Maureen Duffy, *The Erotic World of Faery* (Hodder & Stoughton, 1972)

T.S. Eliot, *Collected Poems and Plays* (Faber & Faber, 1969)

Northrop Frye, *An Anatomy of Criticism* (Princeton, 1957)

Stephen Greenblatt, *Will in the World* (Jonathan Cape, 2004)

Carl Jung quoted in *Psyche and Symbolism in Shakespeare* by Alex Aronson (Indiana University Press, 1972)

Jan Kott, *Shakespeare Our Contemporary* (Methuen, 1964)

Francis Meres quoted in *Introducing Shakespeare* by G.B. Harrison (Penguin, 1966)

John Middleton Murry, *Shakespeare* (Jonathan Cape, 1935)

Ovid, *Metamorphoses*, translated by Mary M. Innes (Penguin, 1971)

M.M. Reese, *Shakespeare: His World and His Work* (Hodder, 1980)

A.L. Rowse, *Shakespeare the Elizabethan* (Weidenfeld & Nicolson, 1977)

Ed. Martin Seymour-Smith, *Shakespeare's Sonnets* (Greenwich Exchange, 2001)

Stanley Wells, Introduction to The New Penguin Shakespeare edition of *A Midsummer Night's Dream*, 1967

Edition used for this study is *The New Penguin Shakespeare* mentioned above.

GREENWICH EXCHANGE BOOKS

STUDENT GUIDE LITERARY SERIES

The Greenwich Exchange Student Guide Literary Series is a collection of critical essays of major or contemporary serious writers in English and selected European languages. The series is for the student, the teacher and 'common readers' and is an ideal resource for libraries. The *Times Educational Supplement* praised these books, saying, "The style of [this series] has a pressure of meaning behind it. Readers should learn from that … If art is about selection, perception and taste, then this is it."

(ISBN prefix 1-871551- applies)
All books are paperbacks unless otherwise stated

The series includes:
W.H. Auden by Stephen Wade (36-6)
Honoré de Balzac by Wendy Mercer (48-X)
William Blake by Peter Davies (27-7)
The Brontës by Peter Davies (24-2)
Robert Browning by John Lucas (59-5)
Lord Byron by Andrew Keanie (83-9)
Samuel Taylor Coleridge by Andrew Keanie (64-1)
Joseph Conrad by Martin Seymour-Smith (18-8)
William Cowper by Michael Thorn (25-0)
Charles Dickens by Robert Giddings (26-9)
Emily Dickinson by Marnie Pomeroy (68-4)
John Donne by Sean Haldane (23-4)
Ford Madox Ford by Anthony Fowles (63-3)
The Stagecraft of Brian Friel by David Grant (74-9)
Robert Frost by Warren Hope (70-6)
Thomas Hardy by Sean Haldane (33-1)
Seamus Heaney by Warren Hope (37-4)
Joseph Heller by Anthony Fowles (84-6)
Gerard Manley Hopkins by Sean Sheehan (77-3)
James Joyce by Michael Murphy (73-0)
Laughter in the Dark – The Plays of Joe Orton by Arthur Burke (56-0)
Philip Larkin by Warren Hope (35-8)
Poets of the First World War by John Greening (79-X)
Philip Roth by Paul McDonald (72-2)
Shakespeare's *A Midsummer Night's Dream* by Matt Simpson (90-0)
Shakespeare's *Macbeth* by Matt Simpson (69-2)

Shakespeare's *Othello* by Matt Simpson (71-4)
Shakespeare's *The Tempest* by Matt Simpson (75-7)
Shakespeare's *Twelfth Night* by Matt Simpson (86-2)
Shakespeare's **Non-Dramatic Poetry** by Martin Seymour-Smith (22-6)
Shakespeare's **Sonnets** by Martin Seymour-Smith (38-2)
Shakespeare's *The Winter's Tale* by John Lucas (80-3)
Tobias Smollett by Robert Giddings (21-8)
Dylan Thomas by Peter Davies (78-1)
Alfred, Lord Tennyson by Michael Thorn (20-X)
William Wordsworth by Andrew Keanie (57-9)
W.B. Yeats by John Greening (34-X)

LITERATURE & BIOGRAPHY

Matthew Arnold and 'Thyrsis' *by Patrick Carill Connolly*
Matthew Arnold (1822-1888) was a leading poet, intellect and aesthete of
the Victorian epoch. He is now best known for his strictures as a literary
and cultural critic, and educationist. After a long period of neglect, his
views have come in for a re-evaluation. Arnold's poetry remains less well
known, yet his poems and his understanding of poetry, which defied the
conventions of his time, were central to his achievement.
The author traces Arnold's intellectual and poetic development, showing
how his poetry gathers its meanings from a lifetime's study of European
literature and philosophy. Connolly's unique exegesis of 'Thyrsis' draws
upon a wide-ranging analysis of the pastoral and its associated myths in
both classical and native cultures. This study shows lucidly and in detail
how Arnold encouraged the intense reflection of the mind on the subject
placed before it, believing in " … the all importance of the choice of the
subject, the necessity of accurate observation; and subordinate character
of expression."
Patrick Carill Connolly gained his English degree at Reading University
and taught English literature abroad for a number of years before returning
to Britain. He is now a civil servant living in London.
2004 • 180 pages • ISBN 1-871551-61-7

The Author, the Book and the Reader *by Robert Giddings*
This collection of essays analyses the effects of changing technology and
the attendant commercial pressures on literary styles and subject matter.
Authors covered include Charles Dickens, Tobias Smollett, Mark Twain,
Dr Johnson and John le Carré.
1991 • 220 pages • illustrated • ISBN 1-871551-01-3

Aleister Crowley and the Cult of Pan *by Paul Newman*
Few more nightmarish figures stalk English literature than Aleister Crowley
(1875-1947), poet, magician, mountaineer and agent provocateur. In this
groundbreaking study, Paul Newman dives into the occult mire of Crowley's
works and fishes out gems and grotesqueries that are by turns ethereal,
sublime, pornographic and horrifying. Like Oscar Wilde before him,
Crowley stood in "symbolic relationship to his age" and to contemporaries
like Rupert Brooke, G.K. Chesterton and the Portuguese modernist,
Fernando Pessoa. An influential exponent of the cult of the Great God Pan,
his essentially 'pagan' outlook was shared by major European writers as
well as English novelists like E.M. Forster, D.H. Lawrence and Arthur
Machen.
Paul Newman lives in Cornwall. Editor of the literary magazine *Abraxas*,
he has written over ten books.
2004 • 222 pages • ISBN 1-871551-66-8

John Dryden *by Anthony Fowles*
Of all the poets of the Augustan age, John Dryden was the most worldly.
Anthony Fowles traces Dryden's evolution from 'wordsmith' to major poet.
This critical study shows a poet of vigour and technical panache whose art
was forged in the heat and battle of a turbulent polemical and pamphleteering
age. Although Dryden's status as a literary critic has long been established,
Fowles draws attention to his neglected achievements as a translator of
poetry. He deals also with the less well-known aspects of Dryden's work –
his plays and occasional pieces.
Born in London and educated at the Universities of Oxford and Southern
California, Anthony Fowles began his career in film-making before
becoming an author of film and television scripts and more than twenty
books. Readers will welcome the many contemporary references to novels
and film with which Fowles illuminates the life and work of this decisively
influential English poetic voice.
2003 • 292 pages • ISBN 1-871551-58-7

The Good That We Do *by John Lucas*
John Lucas' book blends fiction, biography and social history in order to
tell the story of his grandfather, Horace Kelly. Headteacher of a succession
of elementary schools in impoverished areas of London, 'Hod' Kelly was
also a keen cricketer, a devotee of the music hall, and included among his
friends the great trade union leader Ernest Bevin. In telling the story of his
life, Lucas has provided a fascinating range of insights into the lives of
ordinary Londoners from the First World War until the outbreak of the
Second World War. Threaded throughout is an account of such people's

hunger for education, and of the different ways government, church and educational officialdom ministered to that hunger. *The Good That We Do* is both a study of one man and of a period when England changed, drastically and forever.

John Lucas is Professor Emeritus of the Universities of Loughborough and Nottingham Trent. He is the author of numerous works of a critical and scholarly nature and has published seven collections of poetry.

2001 • 214 pages • ISBN 1-871551-54-4

In Pursuit of Lewis Carroll *by Raphael Shaberman*

Sherlock Holmes and the author uncover new evidence in their investigations into the mysterious life and writing of Lewis Carroll. They examine published works by Carroll that have been overlooked by previous commentators. A newly-discovered poem, almost certainly by Carroll, is published here.

Amongst many aspects of Carroll's highly complex personality, this book explores his relationship with his parents, numerous child friends, and the formidable Mrs Liddell, mother of the immortal Alice. Raphael Shaberman was a founder member of the Lewis Carroll Society and a teacher of autistic children.

1994 • 118 pages • illustrated • ISBN 1-871551-13-7

Liar! Liar!: Jack Kerouac – Novelist *by R.J. Ellis*

The fullest study of Jack Kerouac's fiction to date. It is the first book to devote an individual chapter to every one of his novels. *On the Road*, *Visions of Cody* and *The Subterraneans* are reread in-depth, in a new and exciting way. *Visions of Gerard* and *Doctor Sax* are also strikingly reinterpreted, as are other daringly innovative writings, like 'The Railroad Earth' and his "try at a spontaneous *Finnegans Wake*" – *Old Angel Midnight*. Neglected writings, such as *Tristessa* and *Big Sur*, are also analysed, alongside better-known novels such as *Dharma Bums* and *Desolation Angels*.

R.J. Ellis is Senior Lecturer in English at Nottingham Trent University.

1999 • 294 pages • ISBN 1-871551-53-6

Musical Offering *by Yolanthe Leigh*

In a series of vivid sketches, anecdotes and reflections, Yolanthe Leigh tells the story of her growing up in the Poland of the 1930s and the Second World War. These are poignant episodes of a child's first encounters with both the enchantments and the cruelties of the world; and from a later time, stark memories of the brutality of the Nazi invasion, and the hardships of student life in Warsaw under the Occupation. But most of all this is a record of inward development; passages of remarkable intensity and simplicity describe the girl's response to religion, to music, and to her discovery of philosophy.

Yolanthe Leigh was formerly a Lecturer in Philosophy at Reading University.

2000 • 56 pages • ISBN: 1-871551-46-3

Norman Cameron *by Warren Hope*
Norman Cameron's poetry was admired by W.H. Auden, celebrated by Dylan Thomas and valued by Robert Graves. He was described by Martin Seymour-Smith as, "one of ... the most rewarding and pure poets of his generation ..." and is at last given a full-length biography. This eminently sociable man, who had periods of darkness and despair, wrote little poetry by comparison with others of his time, but it is always of a consistently high quality – imaginative and profound.

2000 • 220 pages • illustrated • ISBN 1-871551-05-6

POETRY

Adam's Thoughts in Winter *by Warren Hope*
Warren Hope's poems have appeared from time to time in a number of literary periodicals, pamphlets and anthologies on both sides of the Atlantic. They appeal to lovers of poetry everywhere. His poems are brief, clear, frequently lyrical, characterised by wit, but often distinguished by tenderness. The poems gathered in this first book-length collection counter the brutalising ethos of contemporary life, speaking of, and for, the virtues of modesty, honesty and gentleness in an individual, memorable way.

2000 • 46 pages • ISBN 1-871551-40-4

Baudelaire: Les Fleurs du Mal *Translated by F.W. Leakey*
Selected poems from *Les Fleurs du Mal* are translated with parallel French texts and are designed to be read with pleasure by readers who have no French as well as those who are practised in the French language.

F.W. Leakey was Professor of French in the University of London. As a scholar, critic and teacher he specialised in the work of Baudelaire for 50 years and published a number of books on the poet.

2001 • 152 pages • ISBN 1-871551-10-2

'The Last Blackbird' and other poems by Ralph Hodgson *edited and introduced by John Harding*
Ralph Hodgson (1871-1962) was a poet and illustrator whose most influential and enduring work appeared to great acclaim just prior to, and during, the First World War. His work is imbued with a spiritual passion for

the beauty of creation and the mystery of existence. This new selection brings together, for the first time in 40 years, some of the most beautiful and powerful 'hymns to life' in the English language.

John Harding lives in London. He is a freelance writer and teacher and is Ralph Hodgson's biographer.

2004 • 70 pages • ISBN 1-871551-81-1

Lines from the Stone Age *by Sean Haldane*

Reviewing Sean Haldane's 1992 volume *Desire in Belfast*, Robert Nye wrote in *The Times* that "Haldane can be sure of his place among the English poets." This place is not yet a conspicuous one, mainly because his early volumes appeared in Canada, and because he has earned his living by other means than literature. Despite this, his poems have always had their circle of readers. The 60 previously unpublished poems of *Lines from the Stone Age* – "lines of longing, terror, pride, lust and pain" – may widen this circle.

2000 • 52 pages • ISBN 1-871551-39-0

Martin Seymour-Smith – Collected Poems 1943-1993 *edited by Peter Davies* (180pp)

To the general public Martin Seymour-Smith (1928-1998) is known as a distinguished literary biographer, notably of Robert Graves, Rudyard Kipling and Thomas Hardy. To such figures as John Dover Wilson, William Empson, Stephen Spender and Anthony Burgess, he was regarded as one of the most independently-minded scholars of his generation, through his pioneering critical edition of Shakespeare's *Sonnets*, and his magisterial *Guide to Modern World Literature*.

To his fellow poets, Graves, James Reeves, C.H. Sisson and Robert Nye – he was first and foremost a poet. As this collection demonstrates, at the centre of the poems is a passionate engagement with Man, his sexuality and his personal relationships.

2005 • 182 pages • ISBN 1-871551-47-1

Shakespeare's Sonnets *by Martin Seymour-Smith*

Martin Seymour-Smith's outstanding achievement lies in the field of literary biography and criticism. In 1963 he produced his comprehensive edition, in the old spelling, of *Shakespeare's Sonnets* (here revised and corrected by himself and Peter Davies in 1998). With its landmark introduction and its brilliant critical commentary on each sonnet, it was praised by William Empson and John Dover Wilson. Stephen Spender said of him "I greatly admire Martin Seymour-Smith for the independence of his views and the great interest of his mind"; and both Robert Graves and Anthony Burgess described him as the leading critic of his time. His exegesis of the *Sonnets* remains unsurpassed.

2001 • 194 pages • ISBN 1-871551-38-2

The Rain and the Glass *by Robert Nye*
When Robert Nye's first poems were published, G.S. Fraser declared in the *Times Literary Supplement*: "Here is a proper poet, though it is hard to see how the larger literary public (greedy for flattery of their own concerns) could be brought to recognize that. But other proper poets – how many of them are left? – will recognize one of themselves."

Since then Nye has become known to a large public for his novels, especially *Falstaff* (1976), winner of the Hawthornden Prize and The Guardian Fiction Prize, and *The Late Mr Shakespeare* (1998). But his true vocation has always been poetry, and it is as a poet that he is best known to his fellow poets. "Nye is the inheritor of a poetic tradition that runs from Donne and Ralegh to Edward Thomas and Robert Graves," wrote James Aitchison in 1990, while the critic Gabriel Josipovici has described him as "one of the most interesting poets writing today, with a voice unlike that of any of his contemporaries".

This book contains all the poems Nye has written since his *Collected Poems* of 1995, together with his own selection from that volume. An introduction, telling the story of his poetic beginnings, affirms Nye's unfashionable belief in inspiration, as well as defining that quality of unforced truth which distinguishes the best of his work: "I have spent my life trying to write poems, but the poems gathered here came mostly when I was not."

2005 • 132 pages • ISBN 1-871551-41-2

Wilderness *by Martin Seymour-Smith*
This is Martin Seymour-Smith's first publication of his poetry for more than twenty years. This collection of 36 poems is a fearless account of an inner life of love, frustration, guilt, laughter and the celebration of others. He is best known to the general public as the author of the controversial and bestselling *Hardy* (1994).

1994 • 52 pages • ISBN 1-871551-08-0

BUSINESS

English Language Skills *by Vera Hughes*
If you want to be sure, (as a student, or in your business or personal life), that your written English is correct, this book is for you. Vera Hughes' aim is to help you to remember the basic rules of spelling, grammar and

punctuation. 'Noun', 'verb', 'subject', 'object' and 'adjective' are the only technical terms used. The book teaches the clear, accurate English required by the business and office world. It coaches acceptable current usage and makes the rules easier to remember.

Vera Hughes was a civil servant and is a trainer and author of training manuals.

2002 • 142 pages • ISBN 1-871551-60-9

The Essential Accounting Dictionary of Key Financial Terms
by Linda Hodgson

This is a key aide for students seeking examination success in Accounting A-Level and GNVQ Advanced Business. It results from work with teachers and students and addresses common difficulties. Straightforward, easy to read definitions of key financial terms – which form the basis of understanding and better performance at tests and examination. There is a multiple choice quiz to crosscheck how much the student knows.

Linda Jane Hodgson, graduate in History and Politics, is a former Tax Inspector and qualified teacher. Professionally, she also advised accounting firms on taxation. She now teaches business and finance at a London college.

1999 • 150 pages • ISBN 1-871551-50-1